PEYTON MANNING
LEADER OF THE BRONCOS

THE DENVER POST

Peyton Manning waits behind his Broncos teammates before taking the field for the second half against the Carolina Panthers on Nov. 11, 2012 in Charlotte. *Photo by Joe Amon*

This book is available in quantity at special discounts for your group or organization.
For further information, contact:

Triumph Books LLC
814 North Franklin Street
Chicago, Illinois 60610
Phone: (312) 337-0747
www.triumphbooks.com

Printed in U.S.A.
ISBN: 978-1-60078-863-5

The Denver Post
Writers: Mike Klis, Mark Kiszla and Woody Paige
Editors: Scott Monserud, Meghan Lyden and David Wright
Front cover photo by Steve Nehf. Back cover photo by Tim Rasmussen.

Content packaged by Mojo Media, Inc.
Joe Funk: Editor
Jason Hinman: Creative Director

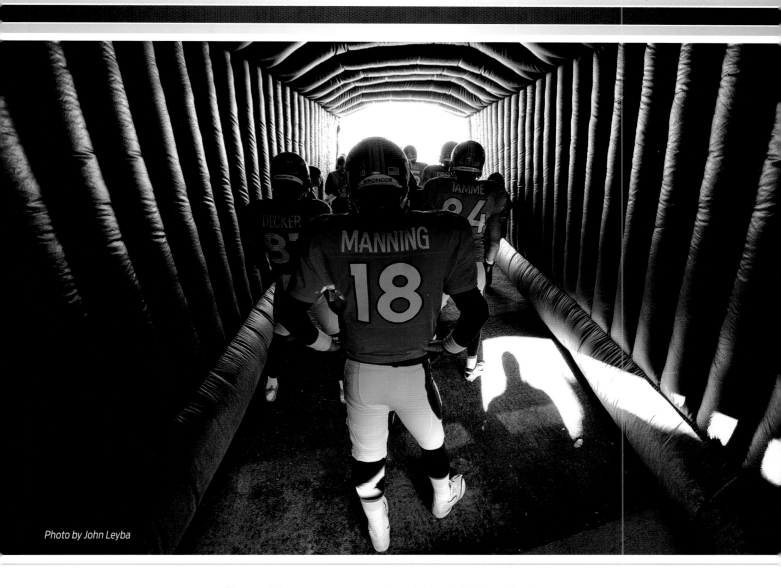

Photo by John Leyba

CONTENTS

INTRODUCTION

For more than a decade, Peyton Manning and the Broncos were successful franchises operating in parallel universes.

Manning for the first 13 years of his NFL career was The Franchise for the Indianapolis Colts. He set single-season passing standards, approached career records, gyrated his limbs while calling plays at the line of the scrimmage, and led all sports figures in amusing commercials.

Manning broke into the NFL in 1998, the same year the Broncos, behind a retiring quarterback named John Elway, won their second consecutive Super Bowl title. The Broncos would continue to win their share during the regular season, but never got far in the postseason, twice getting obliterated by Manning's Colts.

It wasn't until Manning and the Broncos each fell on hard times that they merged to form a happy union. With the Broncos downtrodden from a brief and unfortunate term under Josh McDaniels, owner Pat Bowlen lured Elway out of retirement to lead the football operations department.

Elway watched confoundedly as Tim Tebow magically led the Broncos to an AFC West title in 2011, but ultimately decided if his team was to

take that next step to the Super Bowl, he would need to take a chance on a wounded, wizened, but hardly wilting quarterback in Manning.

After missing his 14th season to recover from four neck surgeries, Manning was set loose to free agency in March 2012 by the Colts.

After a whirlwind recruiting tour, Manning and Elway reached agreement on a five-year, $96 million contract on March 20, 2012. Despite questions about Manning's ability to properly grip the ball and his overall arm strength, he was superb in his first season with the Broncos. In terms of the regular season, it exceeded expectations.

The Broncos finished 13-3 to earn the No. 1 seed in the AFC playoffs. Manning nearly won his unprecedented fifth MVP award, finishing a close second to Minnesota running back Adrian Peterson. Statistically, it was the second-best season of Manning's career as he threw for 4,659 yards, 37 touchdowns and only 11 interceptions. The Broncos finished the season with an 11-game winning streak and began the playoffs with a first-round bye.

All was swell until a frigid January day at Sports Authority Field at Mile High when the

Baltimore Ravens used a last-second, 70-yard touchdown pass to tie the second-round playoff game in regulation, then worked off an interception thrown by Manning to win 38-35 in double overtime.

The Ravens went on to win the Super Bowl. The Broncos and their fan base were disconsolate until the new NFL business season began in March, 2013. This is when Elway and coach John Fox secured star slot receiver Wes Welker and guard Louis Vasquez from free agency and later

added defensive tackle Sylvester Williams and running back Montee Ball in the draft.

Those reinforcements, coupled with rival New England losing Welker and star tight end Aaron Hernandez, who was arrested on first-degree murder charges in late June, make the Broncos the favorite to represent the AFC in Super Bowl XLVIII. It's the first time a Super Bowl will be held in a cold-weather, outdoor venue.

Who better than the Broncos from Denver to play there? ◼

Peyton Manning and John Elway talk on the sideline during the Broncos' 37-6 win over the Oakland Raiders at Sports Authority Field at Mile High on Sept. 30. 2012. *Photo by Joe Amon*

CHAPTER 1

LEADER OF THE BRONCOS

Peyton Manning hands the ball off to Knowshon Moreno during the Broncos' 2012 season opener against the Pittsburgh Steelers. The Broncos won 31-19 in Manning's regular season debut as a Bronco. *Photo by John Leyba*

READY TO WIN

Prepared Manning Eager to Lead Reloaded Broncos to Greater Heights in 2013

They'll get over it. Broncos fans might continue to dwell on the demoralizing way the 2012 season ended. The local media might become a constant source of nightmarish reminders.

Joe Flacco threw the ball how far? Rahim Moore stumbled backwards with how much time left? For the Broncos' players and coaches, though, there will be no problem putting that 38-35 double-overtime playoff loss to Baltimore behind him. They've moved on to 2013.

The Broncos will carry on because the most important person on this team is almost demented in his love for the process. Peyton Manning so much loves the preparation, the result is almost anticlimactic to him. When Manning won his one Super Bowl for the Indianapolis Colts after the 2006 season, he seemed far more relieved than exuberant.

He was thankful that the film study, the game planning, the dinners with teammates, the meetings, the practices, the attention to detail and more practice had all paid off.

That's the stuff that gets Manning out of bed at an absurdly early morning hour each day. Win it all, as Manning did in 2006? That's nice. Now, let's go to work.

Lose in devastating fashion to the Baltimore Ravens? That stinks. Now, let's go to work.

"I know this is the time when people talk about expectations," Manning said after the Broncos' final minicamp workout in mid-June. "But I like to go in phases along the way."

After Flacco's 50-yard rainbow over Moore's head became a 70-yard, game-tying touchdown pass to Jacoby Jones with a mere 31 seconds remaining in regulation — the signature play in the Ravens' Super Bowl run — the Broncos wouldn't have been blamed if they lacked motivation in doing it all over again for 2013.

They had finished the 2012 season with an 11-game winning streak. And none of those victories were nail-biters. Entering the AFC postseason, the Broncos were clearly the team to beat. They earned the No. 1 seed and home-field advantage throughout the conference playoffs. After a bye week, the Broncos were leading Baltimore 35-28 with seconds remaining in their second playoff game at Sports Authority Field at Mile High.

Broncos fans showed their appreciation for Peyton Manning before the Broncos took the field to take on the Kansas City Chiefs in Kansas City on Nov. 25, 2012. *Photo by John Leyba*

Then came Flacco's Fling, a Manning interception late in the first overtime quarter, and a lengthy Baltimore field goal in the second overtime.

After that bitter defeat, Broncos owner Pat Bowlen said in an interview with The Denver Post that he wouldn't mind bringing the nucleus of the team back the next year and try it all over again.

"A lot of those guys are going to be back," Bowlen said on Jan. 13, the day after his team's season ended. "Some of them won't be back, some will go to other teams or whatever, but I'm very comfortable that the nucleus of this football team will be back."

Given two more months to reflect, Bowlen was re-minded how the man he has forever entrusted, John Elway, is not one to wait to react. Elway makes it happen.

When Elway was a Broncos quarterback, he gave Bowlen many an exhilarating victory through his let-'er-rip, fourth quarter comebacks. Thirteen years after Elway retired as a player, Bowlen brought him back to the NFL to run his football operations department.

After luring Manning, the most decorated player in NFL free-agent history, to the Broncos before the 2012 season, Elway sought to reinforce the players around his quarterback for 2013.

His first move was to add up-front protection. By signing right guard Louis Vasquez to a four-year, $23.5 million contract, the Broncos not only added strength to Manning's front line, but weakened the protection for nemesis Philip Rivers, the Chargers' quarterback.

Vasquez was signed within hours after the 2013 NFL business season opened on March 12. The next day, the Broncos jolted the NFL nation by signing Wes Welker,

arguably the best slot receiver in league history, away from the mighty New England Patriots.

The Broncos, good enough to finish No. 2 in the league in scoring in 2012 thanks largely to Manning and his terrific young receiving duo of Demaryius Thomas and Eric Decker, appeared loaded.

"They are all saying the same thing: 'You guys are stacked over there,'" said cornerback Dominique-Rodgers Cromartie, another of the Broncos' free-agent signings in March.

Elway didn't stop tweaking his roster with free agency. The draft brought defensive tackle Sylvester Williams in the first round and Montee Ball in the second.

There was one troubling hic-cup in the Broncos' off-season plan. Hic-cup? Make that the great Fax Fiasco. The Broncos lost defensive end Elvis Dumervil, one of the top pass rushers in the league, to free agency and the dreaded Ravens after the documents to a revised contract didn't get transferred in time to meet the league's deadline.

Then the 2013 NFL schedule came out and — wouldn't you know it — the first game in the entire league will be Broncos vs. Ravens on Sept. 5 at Sports Author-ity Field. The last time these two teams met, the Ravens were prancing off the frozen turf elated while the slunk-shouldered Broncos exited in sorrow. The Broncos won't be downtrodden come kickoff on Sept. 5.

They're rather looking forward to it. "You keep giving yourself opportunities," Manning said. "I like to be in the arena. I like to be in the mix. We were in the mix last year. We want to be back in it this year but we've still got a lot of work to do. This is a totally different season than last year, but hopefully we give ourselves a chance." ■

Broncos coach John Fox congratulates Peyton Manning after the Broncos scored a touchdown against the San Diego Chargers on Nov. 18, 2012. Expectations for 2013 are high after the Broncos finished the regular season 13-3 in Manning's first year in Denver. *Photo by Steve Nehf*

WILD RIDE ENDS IN DENVER

Manning's Arrival Sparks Broncos' Success, Hopes for Future

It all began with The Great Toyota Sequoia Chase.

Peyton Manning, the NFL's only four-time MVP and among the all-time greatest quarterbacks, had arrived by the private plane of Broncos owner Pat Bowlen and was on his way to the Broncos' Dove Valley headquarters.

Could this be? Could the Broncos really be bringing in Manning to be their quarterback? A television helicopter was among the hundreds of thousands along the Front Range that wanted to know.

As Manning and a Broncos' contingent, led by football operations boss John Elway and coach John Fox, climbed into the sports utility vehicle owned and driven by the team's do-everything assistant Fred Fleming on a Friday afternoon, a Denver and national cable audience was spellbound.

The whirlwind visit with Manning was a clandestine arrangement until the shroud of secrecy was pulled back as the free-agent prize sat alone in Bowlen's plane on a runway in Stillwater, Okla.

On March 9, 2012 Elway, John Fox, quarterbacks coach Adam Gase, then general manager Brian Xanders and then offensive coordinator Mike McCoy flew on Bowlen's plane to Stillwater. They had dinner that night with quarterback prospect Brandon Weeden, who was to perform in Oklahoma State's pro-day workout the next morning.

As the Broncos' contingent sat down to dinner, Bowlen's plane was flown to South Florida, where Manning and his family have a condominium.

The next morning, Elway and his Broncos group watched Weeden while Manning was flown from Miami to Stillwater.

Meanwhile, Bowlen had taken a redeye commercial flight from Hawaii, where he keeps an offseason home, to Denver. Make no mistake, Bowlen had his priorities in order.

The Broncos' group joined Manning on the plane in Stillwater, then flew to Centennial Airport near the team's training facility. Manning had to walk only a few feet to the Sequoia.

With a large Denver audience looking on, a TV camera-equipped helicopter followed the SUV carrying Manning until it arrived at the team's headquarters and disappeared into

A Toyota Sequoia picked up Peyton Manning at Centennial Airport on March 9, 2012, and drove him to Broncos headquarters. Broncos head coach John Fox was in the front passenger seat. *Photo by John Leyba*

Bowlen's personal garage. About 50 media and fans were standing outside the gated parking lot and watched the vehicle pull in.

The visit went well. Manning would meet with other teams during his free-agent period, but on March 20 — 10 days after his trip from Florida to Denver with Stillwater, Okla. in between — he called Elway to inform him he had decided to continue his career with the Broncos.

After 13 celebrated seasons with the Indianapolis Colts, Manning brought along significant concerns. Up to 10 teams expressed interest in Manning, based on his past accomplishments. But 22 others declined to pursue him because future performance was in doubt.

Manning had had four neck surgeries. The procedures caused him to miss his entire 14th season at a time when he was about to turn 36 years old.

What he did was answer all his skeptics — none more so than himself — by leading the Broncos to a position where they were favorites to win the Super Bowl entering the 2012 postseason. He led the Broncos to 11 consecutive victories at regular season's end, a run that nearly brought Manning his fifth MVP award.

The playoffs would end in bitter disappointment. Manning had engineered the Broncos to a 35-28 lead with less than a minute remaining in a second-round home game, only to have Baltimore tie it on a 70-yard touchdown pass by Joe Flacco with 31 seconds remaining in regulation. The Ravens then won it in double overtime after an ill-advised Manning pass was intercepted, a turnover that set up the winning field goal.

Still, what Manning did in 2012 was unprecedented. Yes, Joe Montana finished his career in Kansas City after leading the San Francisco 49ers to four Super Bowl titles. Yes, Brett Favre finished in Minnesota after a great run with the Green Bay Packers.

Peyton Manning is congratulated by teammate Demaryius Thomas following the Broncos' win over the Pittsburgh Steelers in Manning's first regular season game as a Bronco. *Photo by John Leyba*

Montana and Favre, though, were healthy as they rewrote the ending to their storybook career. No quarterback had ever come back from four neck surgeries that forced him to miss the entire previous season, as Manning did when he left the Colts and joined the Broncos.

Despite the neck, despite his advanced age, despite playing with a new set of teammates and despite operating a new offense, Manning posted the second-best statistical season of his career. His 105.8 passer rating was computed off 37 touchdowns against only 11 interceptions for 4,659 yards. He completed 68.6 percent of his throws.

During Manning's first season in Denver, he moved past Hall of Famer Dan Marino for second-place on the all-time quarterback list in touchdown passes, passing yards and completions. And, Manning even went past his boss, Elway, for second all-time in wins by a quarterback.

Elway was happy to fall one spot.

Although there was not a happy ending to Manning's first season in Denver, there is the hope, maybe even the expectation, that the Broncos can finish the job as their star quarterback becomes more comfortable in his second season.

Whatever happens, it's already been an incredible journey. From Indy to Stillwater to the well-followed drive in a Toyota Sequoia, the ride that brought Manning to Denver has riveted a region of Bronco fans. ■

Peyton Manning tries to move the ball during the Broncos' loss to the Patriots on Oct. 7, 2002. After starting the season 2-3, the Broncos won their final 11 games to finish 13-3. *Photo by Joe Amon*

CHAPTER 2

Peyton Manning speaks with the media during the March 20, 2012, press conference announcing Manning's signing with the Broncos. *Photo by Joe Amon*

A CALCULATED RISK

PEYTON THROWS, 'LOOKS GREAT'

Stokley Says Manning Passing Like He Did In 2006

If you happened to be walking a dog past a small Castle Rock park the morning of March 10, 2012 and thought, "Gee, that guy throwing the football looks a lot like Peyton Manning," your eyes did not deceive.

That was none other than Peyton Manning throwing passes to his former teammate Brandon Stokley. From about 8:30 to 9:30 on just another gorgeous morning in Colorado, Manning threw about 50 passes to the route-running Stokley. Like Manning, Stokley was a free agent at the time.

"I saw him for three days at Duke and he was the only quarterback (throwing to four or five receivers) and he threw a ton of balls for three straight practices and the guy looked to me like he did when I was there six years ago," said Stokley, the former Broncos receiver who was Manning's teammate with the Indianapolis Colts from 2003-06. "He threw on Saturday here on a little field and maybe because he had some rest, I think he looked better than he had last week."

Between a plane ride from Stillwater, Okla., to Centennial Airport, a six-hour meeting at the team's Dove Valley headquarters and a 2½-hour dinner at Cherry Hills Country Club, Manning spent all the previous day visiting with the Broncos. He spent the night at Stokley's home, in part because he wanted to both rest and get a workout in. Stokley drove him to the Centennial Airport for a 5 p.m. flight to Arizona the next day for a meeting with the Cardinals.

Manning then returned to his offseason residence in the Miami area.

The Broncos and other teams who are pursued the free-agent Manning received some criticism for trying to lure him without watching him work out. But Manning's five-day workout at Duke was filmed, and distributed to teams upon his release March 7 by the Colts.

Manning missed all of 2011 because of complications from multiple neck surgeries.

"People who say the Broncos are crazy for not watching his balls fly, or what are they doing? Those people are dead wrong," Stokley said. "I'll put whatever reputation I have on the line behind that guy right now. He looks great." ■

Peyton Manning gets in some throwing reps at Valor Christian High School in Highlands Ranch, Colorado, on March 26, 2012. After signing with the Broncos, Manning acknowledged that he was still regaining strength after missing the 2011 season. *Photo by John Leyba*

EUPHORIA AND REALITY

Manning Signs With Broncos, Not Yet 100 Percent

Eventually, the thrill subsides, euphoria loses some steam and reality checks in. Peyton Manning is officially the Broncos' quarterback. Incredible. Manning has the Broncos believing they are instantly a Super Bowl contender. Unbelievable.

Manning has a ways to go before he's 100 percent healthy.

Say what?

"I have some strength that I have to get back," Manning said March 20, 2012 in a private conversation with Denver Post reporters.

This is not to scare the Broncos. They're not frightened, because they know. Manning told them everything. The superstar quarterback even may have been the first free agent in NFL history to negotiate terms into his contract that could potentially cost him — and save the team — millions of dollars.

It's no secret Manning has a neck issue. He has undergone four neck surgeries in little more than a year, which is the reason he missed all of 2011 with the Indianapolis Colts and eventually was released to free agency.

Yes, the occasional thought crossed Manning's mind that he might not play again.

"Yeah, you just sort of process it," he said. "I think this process showed that if this was easy, then it would tell you that it didn't really matter that much to me in Indianapolis. All I know is whatever team I'm on, I'm all in with it."

Manning didn't hide his neck condition with teams pursuing him. He put his entire medical history on a disc and gave it to all suitors. He threw for teams interested in signing him, bum neck and all.

While John Elway and Ruston Webster, the front-office bosses for the Broncos and Tennessee Titans, respectively, sent out statements that flattered Manning's throwing audition, the executives, at best, left out some truth and, at worst, told a white lie.

"John said it was great," Manning said. "It wasn't great throwing. It's not supposed to be great because I'm not where I want to be. I just said: 'Here it is, guys. If you're not interested, you're not hurting my feelings. You've got to tell me.' It bothers me that I don't feel the way I want to feel.

Peyton Manning, left, tours Broncos headquarters with head coach John Fox, center, and vice president of football operations John Elway on March 9, 2012. Less than two weeks later, Manning chose to sign with the Broncos. *Photo by John Leyba*

"I have a lot of work to do. I'm not where I need to be."

The Broncos signed Manning to a five-year, $96 million contract, but the story is in the details. Only the first-year $18 million in salary is fully guaranteed. His $20 million salaries for 2013 and 2014 will be guaranteed unless the neck prevents Manning from playing. The fourth- and fifth-year salaries are not guaranteed.

"I'll say this, Peyton was great about giving us protection against his neck," Elway said.

In terms of what football agents, players and accountants would classify as "real money," Manning took a substantial pay cut from his previous deal with the Indianapolis Colts.

He got $26.4 million without playing a down for the Colts last year — 32 percent more than his first-year salary with the Broncos. He was to make $61.8 million after two years with the Colts, $23.8 million more than what the Broncos are planning to pay out through 2013.

"They've got to be protected," Manning said. "That's why the whole medical — I was as open a book as I could be. I told them exactly how I feel, what I was working on. They have to know everything to make their decision.

"Even today, at the last minute, I said, 'John, put it the way you want it.' He and I talked about that from the get-go, on that first visit. You don't want to start off on a bad foot. I kind of argued with them a little bit, on their side. Nobody believes that when you say that. But it's got to be what they're comfortable with."

The reassuring news for Broncos fans is that Manning has been told by three doctors, from three separate medical teams, that he will fully recover. And even if he doesn't, the sentiment among Elway, Broncos owner Pat Bowlen and coach John Fox is

John Elway shakes hands with Peyton Manning during the March 20, 2012, press conference announcing Manning's signing with the Broncos. *Photo by John Leyba*

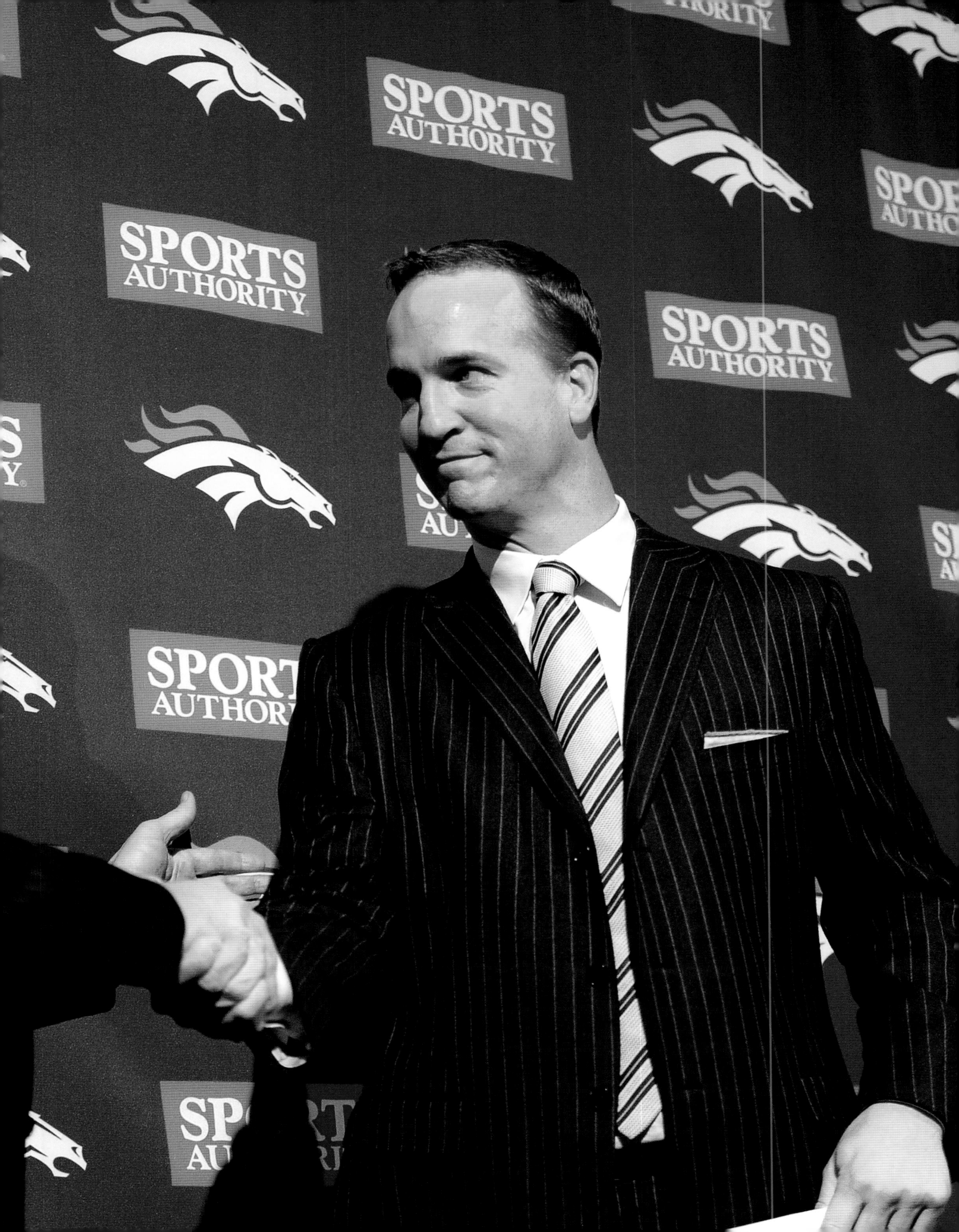
SPORTS AUTHORITY
SPORTS AUTHORITY
SPORTS AUTHORITY

that Manning at 90 percent strength, or even 75 percent strength, is better than almost any other NFL quarterback.

So how did Manning go from a quarterback who needed only 13 seasons to reach No. 3 on the NFL's all-time list in touchdown passes, yards and completions, to one whose cursed number became four? As in four surgeries.

When a neck undergoes four surgeries, it prompts the question: Did somebody mess up the first one?

"No, I went through that history too," Manning said. "I don't think there was a mistake made there. It was just the way it worked out. I haven't played that game on anybody. The Broncos had to make a projection, just like the other teams did. And they all kind of made the same projection. It couldn't happen soon enough for me."

Manning said his most important coaches in the next month, or six months, will be new strength-and-conditioning coach Luke Richesson and long-time trainer Steve "Greek" Antonopulos. The Greek will be consulting with the Colts' trainer to compare notes on how to best to treat Manning's strength and nerve issue.

If Manning recovers in the next three months as well as he's come along in the past three, the Broncos will have the Manning that is among the league's elite quarterbacks.

"The worst question some guys get, they ask these draft choices, 'What are you going to do with the money you just made?'" Manning said. "And they will say they're going to buy this and buy that. And I'm sitting there saying, 'I'm going to try and go earn it.'" ■

Then Broncos general manager Brian Xanders, head coach John Fox, owner Pat Bowlen and executive vice president of football operations John Elway listen as quarterback Peyton Manning during the March 20, 2012, press conference announcing Manning's signing. Manning's contract was reported to pay the quarterback $96 million over five seasons. *Photo by John Leyba*

CHAPTER 3

BACK ON THE FIELD

Peyton Manning calls a play at the line of scrimmage during the Broncos' Aug. 18, 2012, preseason game against the Seattle Seahawks. The game marked Manning's Broncos debut at Sports Authority Field at Mile High. *Photo by Joe Amon*

TRAINING CAMP OPENS

Manning the Man Again After Steady Progress

Let's go back to that mysterious time at Duke University.

It was on the eve of St. Patrick's Day, and Peyton Manning was giving a private audition for the Broncos' brass, coaches and medical team. He threw about 60 passes of various lengths and patterns. Publicly, the Broncos reported Manning threw great.

Privately, while they were encouraged by what they saw, the Broncos' decision makers knew Manning wasn't fully recovered from the neck surgeries that forced the star quarterback to miss the 2011 season.

Fast forward to the Broncos' first training camp practice of the 2012 season. There were 4,372 more fans watching Manning throw on a sunny, warm morning July 26 at Dove Valley than there were four months earlier at the indoor facility at Duke.

How much better did Manning throw on Day One here than he did at Duke?

"That's probably a better question for him," Broncos coach John Fox said. "Because with the type of injury he had, it was a feel thing."

No problem. After Manning's lengthy post-practice news gathering, he was asked about his audition in Durham, N.C. How much better does Manning believe he's throwing?

"It's hard for me to answer that," Manning said. "I'd say it's a better question for Coach Fox."

The first time the Broncos get called for delay of game, you'll know why.

By itself, the question about Manning's Duke performance is benign. It leads to a greater issue, though, regarding Manning in the first comeback season of his career. Based on where he has been, can he get all the way back? Can a 36-year-old veteran rebound from a missed season?

His recovery has been productive — enough for the Broncos to guarantee him $18 million in 2012. The commitment came not without a leap of faith.

The final phases of his recovery were assumed, not 100 percent known.

"I don't think it's a dramatic, noticeable difference between (Duke) and today," Fox said. "I thought he threw pretty well there. I have noticed a difference, but I wouldn't say it was dramatic."

The recovery stage Manning was in during his

Fans look on as Peyton Manning works with the Broncos' offense on July 26, 2012, during the first day of training camp at Dove Valley.
Photo by AAron Ontiveroz

audition at Duke was pretty much where he was during his first organized team activity for the Broncos on May 21.

Manning could throw with zip and accuracy as long as the throws weren't too far downfield. He has come along since.

On the first day of training camp, Manning brought the biggest cheer from the substantial crowd after delivering a 45-yard touchdown pass to Andre Caldwell, who beat his man on a post pattern.

The ball did not flutter or hang. It got there as if it had a deadline to meet.

"He's stronger now than he was in OTAs," Caldwell said. "He's throwing with more zip."

"I don't know if it was first day of OTAs compared to the first day of training camp, but he was on the money today," said Demaryius Thomas, the Broncos' No. 1 wide receiver. "He's throwing the deep ball great."

By his own account, Manning is not all the way back. His account does not include specifics.

"I have certain things I continue to work on and continue to feel like I need to improve," he said cautiously. "I'm certainly not into sharing those with defensive opponents."

The next phase in Manning's recovery comes tomorrow morning, when he'll be padded up for the first time since the Pro Bowl that ended the 2010 season. Maybe he'll take a shove or two.

But regardless of how much further he has to go in his recovery, or how far he has come, it appears Manning is ready to play.

"I think so," Thomas said. "You'll have to ask him, but from what I've seen he's ready."

No sense asking. It will be awhile before the questions disappear anyway. ◼

Manning signs autographs during the first day of Broncos training camp. More than 4,000 fans came out to watch the team practice at Dove Valley. *Photo by AAron Ontiveroz*

PEYTON THE RAINMAKER

Manning's Impact On Denver Felt Not Just On Football Field

The impact of Peyton Manning is not limited to the Broncos.

At the intersection of Arapahoe and Peoria in Centennial, Manning should get free lunches for life with the business he helped bring to the eating establishments down the road from the Broncos' training camp.

"We ran out of food orders three times," said Charles Eckhardt, manager of Chipotle. "I had to borrow like $700 worth of food from stores around the area just to keep up with the orders. Our lunch rush normally goes from 11 to 1, and it's been going all the way to 2 o'clock, 2:30."

Nearby is a Subway, an Einstein's Bagels, Starbucks, Noodles and Company. They've been doing a brisk business for years, anyway.

"But that first week (of training camp), we were out the door," said Michael Young, manager of Subway. "And then we had some trouble with our credit card machine ..."

OK, so maybe Manning only gets free lunch for a year.

It's possible that virtually all businesses within proximity of the Broncos have boomed not because of Manning, but the team. But it's not likely.

The impact of Peyton Manning may not be monopolized by the Broncos, but no entity benefits more.

Utilizing a no-huddle attack that Manning mastered during his 13 previous playing seasons with the Indianapolis Colts, he led the Broncos on one long touchdown drive to end the first quarter in a preseason night game Aug. 18 against the Seattle Seahawks, then artistically engineered a hurry-up drive to end the first half that resulted in a field goal.

Manning's first home performance was mixed as he threw two interceptions. Those two errors, plus a fumble by running back Lance Ball, caused the perfectionist Manning to play longer than expected.

On the touchdown drive, Manning was 4-of-4 for 48 yards. On the field-goal drive, he was 8-of-11 for 77 yards. There were two drops, including one by tight end Jacob Tamme that would have been a touchdown with six seconds remaining in the half.

It had been a while since the crowd at Sports Authority Field at Mile High witnessed this type of passing precision. Manning wound up completing

Media surround Peyton Manning during his weekly press conference on August 23, 2012 at Dove Valley. Manning's first training camp as a Bronco drew increased attention from both media and fans. The Broncos packed in 43,076 fans over 16 practices.
Photo by John Leyba

16-of-23 passes for 177 yards in the half, which ended with the Broncos up 10-9. It wasn't perfect, but it was promising.

While the Broncos typically draw 60 percent to 65 percent of their pre- paid crowd to preseason games, Sports Authority Field was much closer to capacity with the Seahawks in town.

About 80 percent of the stadium was filled when Manning ran out as the anchor to pregame player introductions. The crowd erupted.

The team averaged 17,388 fans for its first three free-admission scrimmages at the stadium from 2009-11. Manning showed up, and the scrimmage Aug. 4 drew an astounding 41,304.

For the training camp practices at Dove Valley, the record attendance before Manning had been 33,071 over 23 practices in 2007. Manning's first camp packed in 43,076 fans with only 16 practices.

"When you have the most popular sport in America, and a fan base that is as passionate and enthusiastic as our fan base is, and now you bring in one of the game's most popular, if not the most popular player, obviously that combination has had a positive impact on the Denver Broncos," said team president Joe Ellis. "I think a lot of that is how Peyton is as a person. They see how he carries himself with style and grace. I think that's an appealing part of his persona that so many people in Denver admire."

And not just here. Manning's new orange-and-blue No. 18 was the NFL's top-selling jersey from April 1 through July 31. Tim Tebow's No. 15 New York Jets jersey ranked No. 3.

Premium importance

It's fairly well known that the Broncos have sold out every home game since 1970, a streak of 325 regular-season games through 2011. Not as well known is those sellouts pertain only to the 65,081 seats in the stadium bowl. The 11,044 premium seats available in the club sections and luxury suites have not always been hot-ticket items in recent years.

Peyton Manning warms up before the Broncos hosted the Seattle Seahawks in an August 18, 2012, preseason game at Sports Authority Field at Mile High. *Photo by AAron Ontiveroz*

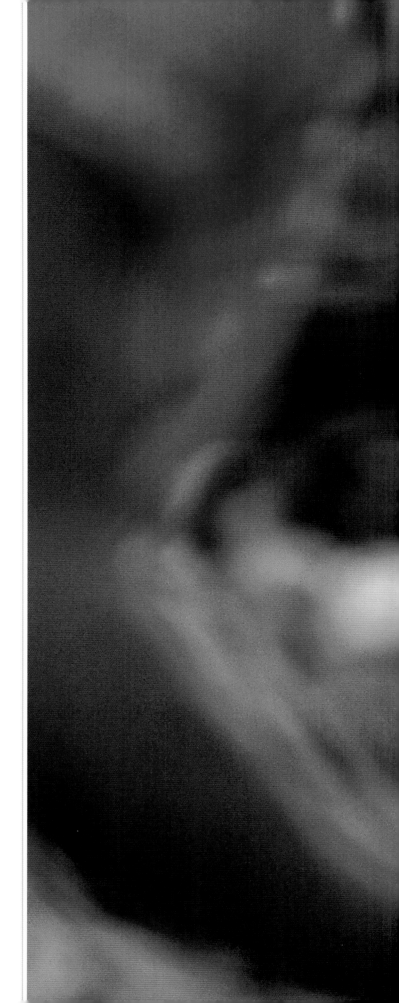

But team officials say there has been a significant uptick in premium seating sales and corporate sponsorships this year.

And to think that only seven months earlier, it didn't seem possible for any athlete to be more celebrated (or notorious) than Tebow. The Broncos' television ratings soared 38 percent in 2011 — albeit from the modern-era low numbers in 2010 that marked the end of the Josh McDaniels disaster.

The momentum of Tebow's magical season no doubt provided the enthusiastic foundation for 2012.

Give credit to Broncos fans, though. Tebow may have fascinated the masses for many reasons. But Manning has captured local imaginations primarily for this reason: He represents realistic hope the Broncos can earn their first Super Bowl title since 1998.

A team does not sign Peyton Manning, who is a four-time league MVP yet 36 years old, with the idea of winning next year.

"I think that's the tone (Broncos owner) Pat Bowlen has set," Ellis said. "And it carries over with John Elway and John Fox, and that trickled down. I think our fans are smart, they're loyal — and they get it."

Fox finally has "the" QB

The impact of Manning sometimes hits Fox as he drives to work in the predawn morning. Fox has been NFL coach for nearly 25 years. His teams' quarterbacks have been Stan Humphries, Neil O'Donnell, Jeff Hostetler, Jake Delhomme and Kerry Collins, all of whom have started in Super Bowls.

But never has Fox had a quarterback close to the quality of Manning. Even if Manning has lost a couple of mph off his fastball, Fox has been around quarterbacks enough to know velocity is well down the list of requirements for great play.

"Nolan Ryan wasn't as fast later in his career as he was early," Fox said. "But he became a better pitcher. Joe Montana lasted as long as he did in the draft (third round, No. 82 overall) because of arm strength. He was pretty good."

The stadium erupts as Peyton Manning runs onto Sports Authority Field at Mile High for his first home preseason game with the Broncos on August 18, 2012. *Photo by Joe Amon*

Maybe even the best all time.

"He's in the discussion," Fox said. "There's a lot to that position. That's why they're so hard to find."

Manning will impact all aspects of the team — the offensive line should find pass blocking easier; the defense should not feel the pressure to hold the opposition to 10 points — but no group has carried a perpetual smile like the receivers.

Eric Decker led the Broncos with 44 receptions in 2011 — which tied with Legedu Naanee and Mike Thomas for 85th in the league. Decker was on pace for 80 catches through the first four full games that Kyle Orton was the quarterback, but the offense went in another direction of Tebow, running and winning.

Can Decker get 80 catches for a winner with Manning as his quarterback in 2012?

"I used to like goal-setting," Decker said. "But when I played baseball I found goal-setting didn't work. Now my mind-set is to prepare for each game, stay healthy and see how it comes out at the end."

Decker is a better route runner in the five months since Manning became his teammate.

"He's helped me understand how to run them better against certain coverages," Decker said.

Turns out, the Broncos have a quarterback who could make a pretty good receivers coach.

"I'm definitely a better route runner because I pay attention to smaller details than I ever did before," said Andre "Bubba" Caldwell. "Sinking your hips, getting your depth, coming out of your breaks, knowing your splits and exactly where to line up."

Oh, yes, lining up. Manning has been known to wave a player into his proper spot.

"That's what he demands out of us, so you've got to do it," Caldwell said.

Which would sound like work except in his next breath, Caldwell said this about the impact of Peyton Manning:

"Football hasn't been this fun for me in a long time." ∎

Ashley Lichtenberg looks at the Broncos shirts available for sale at Where the Buffalo Roam. Sales of Broncos items jumped after Manning joined the Broncos. The quarterback's No. 18 was the NFL's top-selling jersey from April 1 through July 31, 2012. *Photo by Helen H. Richardson*

MIND OF MANNING POWERS DENVER

Broncos Mix QB's Extraordinary Football Brainpower with Their Horsepower

Mike Martz was watching the Broncos practice, not like the television commentator he's practicing to be but as the offensive coordinator he had been.

Specifically, Martz was observing quarterback Peyton Manning, who is new to the Broncos but not to the NFL. Because anticipation is one of Manning's greatest qualities, Martz explained, his greatest adjustment with the Broncos would be becoming familiar with his new set of receivers.

"See that ball right there?" Martz said excitedly.

As if on cue during the Aug. 24 practice, receiver Brandon Stokley sprinted forward from the slot with a defensive player backpedaling close by. Stokley came to a halt, still well covered, and cut to his right. As Stokley moved out of his cut, he gained a step on the defender.

The ball was already airborne. The pass wasn't hurried. Stokley's fingers were not in peril. But as he turned, the ball was coming. Catch, gain of 10 yards.

"He threw the ball right out of the cut," Martz said, marveling at the hardly simple completion. "He doesn't have to gun it. Kurt Warner was like that. Neither one had the strongest arm, but that strong-arm stuff is overrated."

Jeff George could throw a tomato through a locomotive, as Martz put it. But like so many strong-arm quarterbacks, George too often waited for his receiver to come open first. Then he threw. By the time the ball arrives, no matter how fast the ball is humming, the receiver may no longer be open.

Anticipation comes from the mind, which says something about how Manning thinks on the football field. He can see before the image has formed. Stokley wasn't there, yet, but Manning saw him there anyway.

There are times when Manning can tell merely by watching how a linebacker stands whether he is going to drop into coverage or sprint forward on a blitz. Manning can watch how his receiver comes off the line of scrimmage and tell whether he will be open 17½ yards down the field. The Broncos don't have to put a tight end in motion to figure out whether the safety is going to chase, which would indicate man-to-man defense, or drop back into a zone.

For going on a decade or so, Manning has been considered the NFL's smartest quarterback. His cerebral reputation was primarily incited through his demonstrative commands at the line of scrimmage

Peyton Manning looks to pass before being taken down by a Seattle defender during the Broncos' preseason game against the Seahawks on August 18, 2012. *Photo by AAron Ontiveroz*

— well away from the secretive huddle and in front of God, a fan-filled stadium and television audience.

What his many observers may not realize, though, is Manning's mind is not a gift so much as it's been developed. Genius was less a birthright than the product of mental exercise.

"I can't sit here and say he was smarter than everybody else in school, but he was always pretty driven to make good grades," said Archie Manning, Peyton's father. "He wanted to be at the head of the class. So it was work that got him there. He did work at it."

Manning's mind isn't wired in a way where he suddenly gets the urge to draw equations on the chalkboard, like Matt Damon's character in *Good Will Hunting.* Nor is Manning like Russell Crowe's character in *A Beautiful Mind.*

"I was more of a grinder," Manning said. "I used to envy these kids who didn't have to study and get grades."

He did use *Top Gun* characters to call his pass routes during his senior year at Isidore Newman High School in New Orleans.

"We used to number our pass routes — 51, 52 — and he came up to me one day and said, 'Coach, the receivers seem to be having difficulty learning the pass patterns,'" said Peyton's high school offensive coordinator, Frank Gendusa, who later became brother Eli Manning's prep head coach. "And I said, 'OK, Peyton what do you suggest we do?'"

A couple of days later, Newman's offense was calling its pass routes "Maverick," "Goose," "Charlie," "Ice."

If this sounds a tad sophomoric for the buttoned-up, ever-professional Peyton Manning, it's because it was.

"I've always been into word association," Manning said. "Like for instance on a hook route, I came up with Captain. It was our backup quarterback who had the *Top Gun* suggestions. So my suggestions got trumped. Maverick and Goose — there's no word association. At the time, I'd ask, 'Why is this called Maverick?' 'Well, because it is.'"

One of Peyton Manning's skills is the quarterback's ability to adjust to an opponent's defense on a given play. During the Broncos' Aug. 18, 2012, preseason game against the Seattle Seahawks he shouts instructions prior to the snap. *Photo by Steve Nehf*

It may have been nonsense, but Manning went along. Sometimes, a leader is better off going along, even if it rubs against every logical brainwave.

In school, Manning got A's because he studied. How do you ace a spelling test? By going over the word list over and over again. His is a mind heavy on common sense.

Football has its teaching tools too. It has a playbook with X's and O's. And it has a film room where the X's and O's transform into blockers, tacklers and athletes. Manning looks at football film the way a Louvre curator gazes at the Mona Lisa.

"Film study for me was kind of my way of, 'How do you get an edge?'" Manning said. "I'm not going to throw it through them. I can't outrun them. If I can know where they're going before the play starts, I can get some kind of edge. Whether you have an edge or not, at least you think you have one."

Attention to Detail

Science would be far more interesting to more students if the assigned project in lab class was to build the perfect quarterback.

Start with John Elway's arm. It'd be nice to have Michael Vick's legs and Joe Namath's release. Mix in a heavy dose of Joe Montana's poise under pressure. Might as well throw in Tom Brady's good looks because, you know, the perfect quarterback figures to be on his share of magazine covers. There is enough accuracy in the arms of Drew Brees, Aaron Rodgers and Warner to fill an army of perfect quarterbacks.

Manning's mind would be the no-brainer to the perfect-quarterback project.

"I would say so," said Broncos offensive coordinator Mike McCoy. "He's pretty special."

It's not just smarts, though. There is so much gushing about Manning's football intelligence that his physical skills become an afterthought. Manning has prototype quarterback size at 6-foot-5 and 230 pounds strong.

His intelligence may have required work, but his dad told him from a young age that his textbook throwing

motion was natural. Manning didn't throw 399 regular-season touchdown passes during his 13 playing years with the Indianapolis Colts merely by thinking the ball to his receivers. Even if plenty of thought went into it. As former NFL quarterback Phil Simms once told The Denver Post: "I'm the smartest guy there when you line us up for the 100 meters. Big deal. We run the 100 meters, I'm not getting the gold medal."

Still, distinguishing the physical attributes of the all-time best quarterbacks can be debated. Reading a defense before the snap, adjusting to a defensive disguise after the snap, understanding opponent tendencies on third down and vulnerabilities against the no-huddle — this is where Manning is the NFL's valedictorian.

"There's no coach in the NFL who knows more offensive football than he does," Martz said.

And it's not like Manning's mind won't stray to the creative reaches of the brain. In high school, he added shifts and motions to Gendusa's plays. In the NFL, Manning has come up with plays he later saw other teams copy as he was watching film.

"His attention to detail is out of this world," McCoy said. "But he's an out of the box thinker too. The other day he gave a five-minute dissertation to the other three quarterbacks about what he thinks about each of these six or seven concepts."

A Home-Schooled QB

It can't be a coincidence, can it? There has to be a connection between Peyton Manning having such a beautiful football mind and having Archie Manning as his father.

"He sat across the kitchen table from an all-pro, college Hall of Fame quarterback all his life," Gendusa said. "I think Peyton was a little bit ahead of most kids when they come into school to learn football. He knew football. He was around football with his dad from when he was a little bitty kid."

But to hear Archie talk, Peyton and Eli grew up to become premier NFL quarterbacks through happenstance and self-sufficiency.

Peyton Manning is taken down by Seattle linebacker Bruce Irvin during the second quarter of Seattle's 30-10 win over the Broncos in an August 18, 2012, preseason game. After Manning missed the entire 2011 season and underwent four neck surgeries, some questioned the quarterback's durability. *Photo by John Leyba*

"I can't take credit," Archie Manning said. "Football-wise, you have to consider he didn't play organized football for the first time until seventh grade. Seventh grade quarterback is what it is: You hand off and you throw a few passes. Ninth grade is maybe where he started getting into the cerebral part of the game. He did ask me a lot of questions. His questions to me at that time were more about, 'What's my do's and don'ts with the two-minute drill?' Rather than, 'Should I read the middle linebacker and the strong safety on this particular play?' That wasn't happening at age 15 or 16."

Peyton said his father would sit up on the top row during high school games. Archie didn't come to practices. He never gave suggestions to the coaches.

There were throwing sessions with Dad on Sundays — Peyton was 8 when his father played his final NFL season, in 1984. But Archie is more apt to talk about the five all-state receivers he worked with — most notably his oldest son Cooper — than any tip he may have passed on to Peyton or Eli.

Archie insists Peyton got most of his coaching from his coaches. He's getting instruction now from Denver quarterbacks coach Adam Gase. Even though Gase never played quarterback, no one in the past five months has been more inside Manning's mind.

"You have so much on your plate playing quarterback, you need somebody coaching you on your footwork, your mechanics," Manning said. "Adam and I probably spend more time together than anybody else here. We have done intense studies prior to games. We've taken the film from every single angle on throwing motions. What I like about Adam is he is also what I would call a grinder. He has the same goal that I do, which is to play quarterback at as high a level as you can play. So he meets me early, we stay late. We talk on the phone. He's been a big help to me."

Just because Manning knows more offensive football than his coaches doesn't mean he's not coachable. He's smart that way. ▧

Peyton Manning calls a play during the first quarter of the Broncos' Aug. 26, 2012, preseason game against the San Francisco 49ers. Manning threw two touchdown passes in the final preseason tune-up. *Photo by John Leyba*

CHAPTER 4

EARLY STRUGGLES

A dejected Peyton Manning goes over plays with then Broncos offensive coordinator Mike McCoy after going three and out in the third quarter of the Broncos' Week 2 loss to the Atlanta Falcons in Atlanta. *Photo by John Leyba*

GLORIOUS DEBUT

Peyton Manning Leads Denver Broncos to Strong First Win Over Steelers

Hurry-up Peyton. Slow it down, third-down Ben Roethlisberger.

The Broncos' Peyton Manning played quarterback as though he had burning coals beneath those ever-chopping feet. The Pittsburgh Steelers' Roethlisberger played like he was out walking the dog, intent on teaching a few tricks.

It was a stirring game of differing tempo and style. A game of superb quarterbacking. A game of exhaustive defense.

A game that went back and forth.

A game Manning and the Broncos won 31-19, even though they barely touched the ball in the second and third quarters.

"When he did get the ball, and we needed big drives, Peyton came through for us," Broncos defensive tackle Justin Bannan said. "That's what we brought him here for. You watch the way he runs the clock, you watch him be patient, you watch the little things he does, as a defensive player you're standing there with a smile on your face."

The 2012 season opener was played on a perfectly comfortable Sept. 9 evening before a sellout crowd of more than 76,000 at Sports Authority Field at Mile High and a nationally televised audience. It was a game Tracy Porter clinched with a 43-yard interception return for a touchdown at the two-minute warning.

The Broncos won primarily because Manning is back in all his glory. He is the Peyton Manning of old. Despite missing all of 2011 with a neck injury, despite playing with a new team in a new home stadium with new teammates, Manning played quarterback as Michelangelo would paint, as Shakespeare would write, as Fred Astaire would dance.

Manning plays as an artist. He threw his 400th and 401st touchdown passes of his career, Nos. 1 and 2 with the Broncos.

He completed 73.1 percent (19-of-26) of his passes, or 26 percent higher than Tim Tebow's season mark last season, while posting a 129.2 quarterback rating.

Manning did almost all his damage after the team junked its huddle-up, walk-up-to-the-line offense after a scoreless first quarter. In its place came the no-huddle offense. The beauty of the no-huddle is it allows Manning to be in complete charge of the offense from the line of scrimmage.

"I think it made a difference," Manning said of the no-huddle. "I think it gave our offense a little boost and got us in a little rhythm."

Manning led the Broncos back from a 19-14

Peyton Manning takes the field prior to the Broncos' 2012 season opener against the Pittsburgh Steelers on Sept. 9, 2012.
Photo by Joe Amon

deficit early in the fourth quarter. He couldn't lead them back before then because the Broncos' offense seemingly never had the ball.

Roethlisberger's remarkable efficiency on third down — in particular on third-and-long — was reminiscent of the 2005 AFC championship game played in Denver. The Steelers converted eight of their first nine third downs, including five consecutive of at least 7 yards, to defeat Jake Plummer and the Broncos 34-17 on that day. The Broncos haven't come close to the Super Bowl since, although Plummer was back in the stadium on this night, this time as a fan, to see if Manning could get them on their way.

Jake the Snake almost saw Big Ben do it again. When Roethlisberger converted a third-and-2 seconds into the fourth quarter with a 3-yard touchdown pass to Mike Wallace, the Steelers at that point were a ridiculous 12-of-17 on third down.

"It starts with me and Elvis (Dumervil) — we have to do a better job on the pass rush," Broncos linebacker Von Miller said.

Although Miller would get two sacks in the final seconds, with the outcome settled, he was frustratingly close to Roethlisberger several times when it counted, only to see the burly Steeler convert third downs on plays of 18, 13, 12, 11, 10 and 9 yards.

Third downs are clock hoggers. The Steelers had the ball 14 minutes and 24 seconds of the 15-minute third quarter. They had it 9:38 of the second quarter.

After going 20 months and one week since his last regular-season game to finish the 2010 season, Manning waited one more quarter to guide a touchdown drive.

Defense dominated the early play. Neither team ran the ball well. Neither team hit the big play in the passing game.

It wasn't until the well-decorated quarterbacks received the freedom to do what they do best that the game became entertaining.

For Manning, it meant switching from the ponderous huddle-'em-up, establish-the-run offense to the no-huddle starting in the second quarter. The uptick in tempo helped Manning lead a 12-play, 80-yard touchdown drive the Broncos

finished off with a 7-yard TD run by Knowshon Moreno.

During the drive Manning was methodically efficient, completing 6-of-7 passes for 51 yards. No surprise there. He did have two plays, though, that were wonderfully out of character. On one, he scrambled right for a 7-yard gain past the first-down marker. On another, Manning was getting wrapped and thrown down by Steelers linebacker Larry Foote. But as he was falling, Manning dumped an incompletion to Willis McGahee.

Foote fumed at the referee for not blowing the play dead. Instead of second-and-long from the 40, Manning on the next play completed a short pass that set up a third-and-1 at the Pittsburgh 25.

Manning finished off the drive, and the Broncos were up 7-3 with 5:16 remaining in the half. Roethlisberger and the Steelers took up most of it.

On third-and-13 from the 21, Roethlisberger hit Emmanuel Saunders, who free-lanced away from coverage, for a 17-yard gain and first-and-goal at the 4. Two plays later, Steelers tight end Heath Miller outmaneuvered Broncos linebacker Joe Mays to get open for a 4-yard touchdown reception.

"In a first game like that, Ben Roethlisberger's a tough guy to play against because he does extend plays," Broncos coach John Fox said.

Aside from a Manning kneel-down to kill the final seconds of the half, the Broncos had the ball for just one possession in the second quarter. They scored a touchdown on that possession. Yet, the Broncos lost the quarter.

After 8 minutes and 55 seconds of third-quarter game clock, the Steelers had to settle for a 35-yard Shaun Suisham field goal. The Steelers were up 13-7, and the Broncos were finally going to get the ball.

Two plays later, it was 14-13 Broncos. Manning completed a pass to Eric Decker on the right, then with the no huddle, threw a simple receiver screen to Demaryius Thomas on the left. With left guard Zane Beadles throwing a block 20 yards downfield, Thomas went all the way with a 71-yard catch-and-run-and-run-and-run touchdown.

The drive took 36 seconds. ▪

Peyton Manning signals touchdown after his 1-yard pass to Jacob Tamme put the Broncos ahead 22-19 in the fourth quarter. The final score was 31-19 as the Broncos won their season opener. *Photo by John Leyba*

PASSING OF THE TORCH?

Peyton Manning Outdone by Matt Ryan as Broncos Lose 27-21 to Falcons

Maybe, just maybe, the NFL is ready to complete its transition of elite-tier quarterbacks.

Not that Peyton Manning should be harshly judged because he had one unfortunate performance after a missed season with four neck injuries.

But does anyone else see a young Manning in Matt Ryan?

A more mobile Peyton? Ryan was Joe Montana-like cool, Manning-like accurate and Manning-like intelligent in leading the Atlanta Falcons, who defeated the Broncos and error-plagued Manning, 27-21, on Monday night Sept. 17 before a raucous sellout crowd at the Georgia Dome.

Manning threw three interceptions on the Broncos' first three possessions and Denver was unable to recover.

"Anytime you go on the road and you throw three interceptions to put your team in a hole, to put our defense in a hole, and give Atlanta great field position, it's disappointing," Manning said. "Just got to protect the ball batter. … No excuses for me. Poor decisions, I threw the ball into coverage. We battled back and had a chance, but in the end I put our team into too big of a hole."

Ryan is beginning his fifth NFL season. He threw his 100th career touchdown pass in the third quarter. Manning is in his 15th season. Last week, he threw his 400th touchdown pass.

Ryan was way above the grading curve in his first four regular seasons but the postseason has been his albatross. He and the Falcons have lost three consecutive playoff games.

Funny, when Manning was with the Indianapolis Colts, he started 0-3 in the postseason too. In this game, up-and-coming Ryan clearly outplayed the iconic Manning, whose three interceptions were all on throws over the middle.

Denver rallied in the fourth quarter, but never got the ball back with a chance to tie as the Falcons ran out the clock after the Broncos pulled to within six.

The Broncos had four turnovers in their first five possessions.

"A little too much to overcome," said Broncos coach John Fox.

Hurt early when his nervous receivers made crucial drops, Ryan efficiently led the Falcons to touchdowns on his last possession of the first half and second drive in the second half.

"I played with him his first year and you knew right away that Matt Ryan gets it," said Broncos linebacker Keith Brooking. "They've done a real good job of getting weapons around him and building that offense around him."

Manning, meanwhile, had one of those games.

Falcons safety William Moore steps in front of Broncos tight end Jacob Tamme to intercept a Peyton Manning pass in the first quarter of the Broncos' loss to the Falcons in Week 2. Manning threw interceptions on the Broncos' first three possessions.
Photo by John Leyba

What, you thought he would dominate every game after missing all of last season? Comebacks are never easy in the NFL.

For only the second time in his career, Manning threw three interceptions in the first quarter. The other time was during a torrential downpour in San Diego, where on Nov. 11, 2007, he wound up throwing a career-most six picks.

Still, Manning would have led the Colts to victory in that game if not for a missed short field goal in the final seconds by Adam Vinatieri.

When Manning in this game led the Broncos on an 80-yard touchdown drive to end the first half, narrowing the Falcons lead to 20-7, there seemed to be a chance the quarterback's ugly start could be overcome. But the Broncos went three-and-out on their first possession of the second half — a 1-yard completion to Demaryius Thomas and two incompletes — while Ryan combined with Roddy White to smartly execute a 74-yard scoring drive that put Atlanta up 27-7. Manning then led the Broncos on a long scoring drive to make it 27-14 with 11:48 left in the game on Willis McGahee's 2-yard run. McGahee added a late scoring run for the final score.

Wide receiver Brandon Stokley said the offense "is a continuous work in progress. It's something we're going to have to keep working at, the entire season."

Broncos safety Mike Adams said Manning will rebound. "He's going to be all right." Adams said. "I've seen him have games like that before, and he still came back and won them. One more quarter and we win this one."

It was a tough night for the fiery Fox, too. At wit's end with the replacement officials, Fox is beginning to rival San Francisco's Jim Harbaugh as the top bully to the fill-ins. Fox got a pass interference call reversed and an unsportsmanlike penalty flagged against him that was never marked off. Several penalties were seemingly marked with peculiar yardage.

Then again, Broncos right tackle Orlando Franklin came away with a hotly contested recovery on a Knowshon Moreno fumble yet the officials awarded Atlanta the ball. During the tussle for the oblong prize, tempers flared and the pushing match wound up with Fox in the middle of it. Fox was in the middle because he had strayed several yards into the field of play.

The Broncos players reflected their coach's spirit. With Manning's play, and his passes, wobbling, McGahee started running the ball with authority. McGahee had 77 yards rushing on just 11 carries at the half.

On defense, Denver gave the Falcons fits despite poor starting field position. There was so much attention paid to Manning's poor play that the Falcons' offensive ineptitude was almost overlooked. The combination of Denver D tenacity and four dropped Falcon passes — two each by Julio Jones (one that would have been a touchdown) and Tony Gonzalez — kept the Broncos in the game.

It was only 10-0 Falcons after the first quarter even though the Broncos committed four turnovers. On the Falcons' lone touchdown, they needed three Michael Turner rushing plays to go 1 yard. Atlanta only had to go 1 yard because on the Broncos' first possession, Manning's pass intended for tight end Jacob Tamme floated and knuckled into the awaiting arms of Atlanta's William Moore.

The safety returned it 33 yards to the 1.

Finally, both offenses got it going with their final possession of the first half. Ryan started going to No. 3 receiver Harry Douglas, who was working on new Broncos' nickel back Tony Carter, while mixing in mid-range completions to Gonzalez and Roddy White. Carter was replacing the injured Chris Harris.

A 1-yard flip to a wide-open Gonzalez in the back of the end zone gave the Falcons a 20-0 lead with 4:39 remaining in the half.

At that point, Manning became methodical. The Broncos huddled up as a way to slow down their heartbeats. A mix of short passes to Eric Decker and McGahee runs brought the Broncos within scoring distance. A great catch by Thomas, who starred here at Georgia Tech, finished the drive.

On third-and-goal from the 17 and just 16 seconds left in the half, Manning threw to the left side of the end zone where Thomas caught it but appeared to be pushed out of bounds with just one foot down. Until the replay. A slow-motion look revealed Thomas was able to drag his right toe off the turf. The right toe represented his second foot down and the Broncos had a touchdown.

The Falcons went into the locker room up 20-7 but the Broncos were confident that they were the team with the momentum.

Ryan took the momentum back in the third quarter. ■

Peyton Manning throws a pass during the fourth quarter against the Falcons in Week 2. The Broncos scored two fourth-quarter touchdowns, but fell short, 27-21. *Photo by John Leyba*

Peyton Manning gets a pass off moments before taking a hit during the Broncos' Sept. 23, 2012, loss to the Houston Texans. The Texans sacked Manning three times as the Broncos' record fell to 1-2. *Photo by Joe Amon*

Demaryius Thomas breaks away for a short gain in the third quarter of the Broncos' Sept. 30, 2012, game against the Oakland Raiders. Thomas totaled five catches for 103 yards as the Broncos thumped the Raiders 37-6. *Photo by John Leyba*

PEYTON PLAYS WELL, BUT DEFENSE CAN'T KEEP UP

Brady Tops Manning as Patriots Beat Broncos in Track Meet

This was not a game for the weak of kidney.

To have grabbed a beverage from the fridge was to have missed multiple plays, at least one of which no doubt went for a New England first down.

Tom Brady and the New England Patriots defeated Peyton Manning and the Broncos 31-21 on Oct. 7 in a high-tempo exercise at Gillette Stadium that was not so much an NFL game as a track meet of rush into the blocks, short sprints, hurry back to the blocks, sprint a few more yards.

The Patriots built a 24-point lead by playing Road Runner to Denver's frustrated Wile E. Coyote.

"That was fast," said Broncos safety Mike Adams. "They must have had two plays called before they went to the line. That allows them to get up to the line and call the play they want. They had two plays and we started doing that too in the second half when we started to slow it down. But I have to admit, that was pretty fast."

The Broncos made it a game late, thanks to their own no-huddle attack that produced two of Manning's three touchdown passes. But the Broncos never approached the warp speed of the Patriots' offense.

"We can go pretty fast at home if we communicate really well," Brady said.

How fast were the Patriots' going? So fast they were able to get off an astounding 89 plays. So fast they were able to register a team-record 35 first downs. Let's put those 35 first downs into further perspective. Remember in 2007, when the Patriots went 16-0, Brady threw an NFL-record 50 touchdown passes and the offense scored a record 589 points? That team nor any other team in Patriots history registered 35 first downs, as New England did in this game.

"For me, that was the fastest-tempo first half I've been in," said Broncos defensive tackle Justin Bannan.

Keep in mind, this is Bannan's 11th NFL season.

"We have to keep on working on that because that's the way the whole NFL is going now," said Broncos defensive tackle Mitch Unrein. "Everyone is trying to hurry it up and snap the ball."

Brady vs. Manning XIII wasn't a quarterback

Peyton Manning and Broncos head coach John Fox talk things over during a second-quarter timeout during the Broncos' loss to the Patriots on October 7, 2012. *Photo by John Leyba*

duel. It was two guys playing the point, dishing passes on the fast break.

Depending on your point of view, the difference between these two point guards who will someday be enshrined in the Pro Football Hall of Fame is either Brady does a better job of dishing or his teammates do a better job of finishing.

Brady is 9-4 in head-to-head meetings with Manning; 1-0 since the Broncos were brought into this quarterback rivalry.

Certainly, Demaryius Thomas hasn't been finishing. For the second time in two games, Thomas wasted a long pass play from Manning by fumbling the ball away. The Broncos were moving the ball on their first possession against the Patriots when Thomas snatched a Manning pass and was approaching the Patriots' 10 with a 43-yard gain when cornerback Sterling Moore swatted the ball loose from behind. Moore recovered and the Broncos' only chance to dictate the game's tempo was gone.

Brady controlled the game from there. He was 17-of-20 passing in the first half. He destroyed the Broncos' secondary in two games last season using tight ends Aaron Hernandez and Rob Gronkowski. With Hernandez missing Sunday's game because of a bum ankle, Brady and offensive coordinator Josh McDaniels decided to isolate veteran slot receiver Wes Welker against Broncos nickel back Chris Harris and others.

Welker had nine catches by halftime, including an 8-yard touchdown reception that opened the scoring, and finished with 13 receptions.

When it came to converting third downs, though, Brady was less discriminating. On a third-and-14 play — third-and-14! — Brady scrambled right and dumped the ball to running back Danny Woodhead, who shifted, cut and churned for 25 yards. Woodhead later converted a third-and-17 play with a 19-yard run.

For a while, it appeared Manning would be able to keep up. Early in the second quarter, he finished an 80-yard drive with a 1-yard touchdown pass to tight end Joel Dreessen that tied the score at 7-7.

But between the Patriots' relentless offensive tempo wearing down the Denver defense and the Broncos' offense losing rhythm as it stood helplessly watching on the sideline, Dreessen's touchdown marked the start of New England's dominance.

When Brady leaped, landed and shuffled in for a 1-yard touchdown run to finish a 16-play drive that lasted more than six minutes, the Broncos were down 24-7.

A play later, when Manning was sacked by New England linebacker Rob Ninkovich, forcing a fumble that the Patriots recovered just 14 yards from another score, the Broncos were buried. The Patriots turned the turnover into a quick, easy touchdown and a 31-7 lead with less than five minutes remaining in the third quarter.

With their season nearly one-third gone, how to best define the Broncos? They are 2-3 — 0-3 against teams with a winning record. That says the Broncos are not yet good enough to beat real good teams. The Broncos need to hurry, because they're playing the AFC West-leading Chargers in San Diego next week. ■

Peyton Manning shares a moment with New England quarterback Tom Brady after the Patriots' 31-21 win over the Broncos on Oct. 7, 2012. The win upped Brady's record to 9-4 in head-to-head matchups with Manning. *Photo by Joe Amon*

CHAPTER 5

THE STREAK

Peyton Manning throws a touchdown pass to Eric Decker during the Broncos' 38-3 defeat of the Kansas City Chiefs in Week 16. The win was the Broncos' 11th in a row to close the season. *Photo by Joe Amon*

COMEBACK SPARKS WIN STREAK

Broncos Erase 24-point Deficit to Drop Chargers

It seemed as though Peyton Manning was saying it because he had to say it. It was after the New England game the week before and the Broncos fell way behind before making a spirited comeback, only to again fall short in the end. And so Manning was saying what coaches and players always say. "Once again, we did continue to fight and compete in the second half," Manning said.

A leader has to stay positive. Can't let the team get down.

"Which I do think we can build on and have it help us win a game at some point," Manning said.

Yeah, right, Peyton. Here the Broncos were again Monday night, Oct. 15, in a pivotal AFC West game against the rival San Diego Chargers.

The Broncos fell way behind. Way, way behind. Only this time, all that practice at overcoming a large deficit paid off. Manning was brilliant in leading the Broncos to a shocking 35-24 win against the Chargers.

"I'm in shock right now that we just did that," said Broncos defensive tackle Justin Bannan.

"I'm just glad I was part of it. That's one you will remember forever."

The Broncos trailed 24-0 at halftime.

"I've never been part of a comeback like that," said Joel Dreessen, one of the Broncos' two pass-catching tight ends. "Peyton, that guy is so humble. I tried to get him fired up about this. I was shaking him, and saying, 'What do you think about this, man?' All he said was, 'Good job. Good job.'"

Not that 24 down was all that unusual. In losing three previous games, the Broncos were down 20 points in the fourth quarter to Atlanta, 20 points in the fourth to Houston and 24 points late in the third quarter at New England.

The Broncos rallied in each game before losing by six points, six points and 10 points. All that practice at overcoming three touchdown deficits helped the Broncos this time.

"I think so," said Manning. "The guys did understand in the past few weeks that we can score quickly. We are able to come back, it's just a matter of how far we can come back." This time,

Peyton Manning moves under pressure during the Broncos' Monday Night Football matchup with the San Diego Chargers on Oct. 15, 2012. After the Broncos trailed 24-0 at halftime, Manning led the Broncos to 35 unanswered points in the second half. *Photo by Joe Amon*

Manning and defensive back Tony Carter had a 24-0 deficit changed to a 28-24 lead before the game reached the 9-minute mark of the fourth quarter. At one point in the second half, Manning was 13-of-13 for 167 yards and three touchdowns.

"You never can count that guy out," said receiver Brandon Stokley, who made a sensational catch for a 21-yard touchdown with 9:03 remaining to give the Broncos the lead for good. "I've seen it too many times. Everybody in this locker room knows, and we all believe, that when you have him behind the center we can come back from any deficit."

Manning didn't do it all by himself. He was a hero but so were defensive backs Carter and Chris Harris.

Both Carter and Harris were elevated by the absence of right cornerback Tracy Porter. Carter had an interception and 65-yard fumble return for a touchdown. Harris had two interceptions, including a pick six with 2:05 remaining that clinched the game.

"I've been a part of some comebacks and you have to have all three phases contribute," said Manning, whose 47th game-winning drive in the fourth quarter tied Hall of Famer Dan Marino for the all-time NFL lead. "You've got to have a tipped ball or a bounce go your way."

It was potentially a monumental win for the Broncos. For starters it evened their record at 3-3 and left them tied with the 3-3 Chargers for the AFC West lead.

This is a tie that has a feel of the Broncos running away with it.

The first half was a disaster for Denver. It wasn't so much the Chargers stormed the Broncos as much as the Broncos beat themselves. Three Bronco turnovers resulted in 17 Charger points.

The first mistake was the old careful-what-you-wish-for lesson. The Broncos acknowledged Jim Leonhard was a sure-handed punt catcher, but they wanted more return.

So they claimed the explosive Trindon Holliday off waivers. Holliday failed to catch two short punts that gave the Broncos' poor field position and muffed an attempt at a fair catch that gave San Diego the ball at Denver's 17-yard line.

It took Chargers' quarterback Philip Rivers about three series to warm up so Holliday's muff led only to a short field goal.

On the ensuing kickoff, Broncos returner Omar Bolden fumbled. The Chargers' offense went back out there with the ball already in the red zone. This time, Rivers hit tight end Antonio Gates for a 15-yard touchdown pass. It was 10-0.

In the second quarter, with the Broncos struggling to execute their no-huddle offense amid the din at Qualcomm Stadium, Manning finally connected on a deep pass down the middle to Eric Decker, who was open from here to Carlsbad. It appeared Decker would score on the play, but before reaching the Chargers' 40 yard line, the excitement of it all caused him to stumble.

He wound up with a 55-yard gain to the Chargers 30. Nice play, but three plays later, Manning threw a square-in pass to Matt Willis. That was a problem. Willis ran a go route. The ball landed in Quinton Jammer's stomach. He returned it 80 yards for a touchdown.

The Decker stumble may well have been a 14-point play. The three turnovers enabled the Chargers to build a 17-0 lead. The Chargers finally scored a touchdown on their own, although a defensive holding penalty on Broncos rookie linebacker Danny Trevathan did convert a third down. Rivers hit Gates for another touchdown, this one for 11 yards and it was San Diego 24, Broncos nothing but embarrassment.

And then, as they always do, the Broncos rallied. This time, they came all the way back. Manning started the rally on the first series of the second half. He set the Chargers up with three completions in the soft middle of the Chargers'

Broncos safety Chris Harris sprints to the end zone after picking off a Philip Rivers pass in the fourth quarter. Harris' touchdown sealed the Broncos' 35-24 victory. *Photo by John Leyba*

defense to Dreessen for 11, 19 and 10 yards.

That opened up a deep throw to Demaryius Thomas, who easily beat Jammer for a 29-yard touchdown.

After the Manning-to-Thomas touchdown, Rivers was driving into Broncos territory when Denver defensive end Elvis Dumervil got in to swat the ball out of his hand as he attempted to throw. Carter, playing because Porter was left home sick, picked up the ball and raced 65 yards for a touchdown.

Now it was 24-14 and the Chargers were in trouble. Denver's defense finished off a three-and-out with a sack by rookie Derek Wolfe.

On the next drive, Manning mixed in Willis McGahee runs with short passes. But this time, he needed a Manning special. In what may have been the pass of the 2012 season, Manning converted a third-and-16 on the first play of the fourth quarter with a pass down the left sideline to tight end Jacob Tamme.

Tamme ran a sideline-and-up and just as he turned up, the ball was there. The 25-yard gain gave the Broncos the ball at the 25, from where two McGahee runs and two Manning passes to Decker finished the job.

On a swing pass to Decker from the 7, the receiver would not be denied as he bull-rushed a defender into the end zone. Just 1:27 into the fourth quarter, 24-0 was 24-21.

Manning completed the comeback with a 21-yard touchdown to Stokley, a play that was sensational in both pass and catch. The Broncos were up 28-24 with 9:03 remaining.

At that point, Rivers and the Chargers fell apart. Rivers threw his fourth interception, a sideline pass that Harris picked off and returned 46 yards for the clincher.

Manning finished 24-of-30 for 309 yards with the three touchdowns. ■

Then Broncos defensive end Elvis Dumervil celebrates after sacking Chargers quarterback Philip Rivers in the fourth quarter of the Denver's 35-24 win in San Diego.
Photo by Joe Amon

Peyton Manning organizes the Broncos' offense in the huddle during the fourth quarter of Denver's 34-14 win over the New Orleans Saints on Oct. 28, 2012. The win pushed the Broncos record to 4-3. *Photo by John Leyba*

Eric Decker jumps into the stands at Sports Authority Field at Mile High after his 14-yard touchdown reception gave the Broncos a 14-7 second-quarter lead over the New Orleans Saints on Oct. 28, 2012. *Photo by Joe Amon*

Peyton Manning fires up the Broncos' offensive line during the fourth quarter of the Broncos 30-23 win over the San Diego Chargers on Nov. 18, 2012. Manning threw for 270 yards and three touchdowns. *Photo by John Leyba*

Broncos defensive tackle Mitch Unrein (second from left) celebrates with teammates Eric Decker (No. 87), Dan Koppen (No. 67), and Peyton Manning (No. 18) after catching a 1-yard touchdown pass against the Tampa Bay Buccaneers. Manning threw for two more touchdowns in the Denver's 31-23 win on Dec. 2, 2012. *Photo by AAron Ontiveroz*

Peyton Manning takes the field at Baltimore's M&T Bank Stadium before the Broncos took on the Ravens on Dec. 16, 2012. The Broncos defeated the eventual Super Bowl XLVII champions, 34-17. *Photo by Joe Amon*

Peyton Manning completes a pass to tight end Joel Dreessen for a first down during the first half of the Broncos' home win over the Cleveland Browns on Dec. 23, 2012. Manning threw for 339 yards and three touchdowns in Denver's 34-12 win. *Photo by AAron Ontiveroz*

PHASE ONE COMPLETE

Manning Carries Broncos Past Chiefs, Denver Clinches No. 1 Playoff Seed

Now that he's completed the regular-season portion of his remarkable comeback, perhaps the legacy of Peyton Manning should be revisited.

It never was a question of whether he was among the best quarterbacks of all time. That is basically indisputable. The debate is whether he is the best.

Manning's legacy doesn't need a fifth MVP, nice as that would be. It needs a second Super Bowl title ring.

The journey for No. 2 was enhanced Sunday, Dec. 30. Manning was especially sharp, throwing three touchdown passes in the Broncos' name-their-score, 38-3 whipping of the pathetic Kansas City Chiefs before a bundled, but satisfied sellout crowd at Sports Authority Field at Mile High.

In the locker room afterward, Broncos owner Pat Bowlen presented the game ball to his coach, John Fox, who earned his 100th career NFL victory. Fox told his owner he hoped to get him three more before the season is out.

"Coach Fox made a point for us to take a day to reflect on what we have done this season," Manning said. "I know I'll certainly do that. It's been quite a year for me. It's been like no other year I've been through."

The crowd delivered a standing ovation to the Broncos' defense as it moved from the south side to the north between the third and fourth quarters. And the fans chanted "MVP!" for Manning as the final seconds ticked off.

In his first season with the Broncos, Manning set several season franchise records and surpassed numerous NFL milestones. Most important, he helped Denver secure the AFC's No. 1 playoff seed. The Broncos' 11th consecutive victory, coupled with the Houston Texans' second straight loss, means the AFC playoffs will go through Denver.

"The Super Bowl is what it's all about with Peyton," said Broncos cornerback Champ Bailey. "He's such a team guy. Individual awards are great — I'd love to see him get the MVP, but at the same

Peyton Manning scrambles out of the pocket during the Broncos' final regular season game of 2012, a 38-3 thumping of the Kansas City Chiefs. Manning completed 23 of 29 pass attempts in the win. *Photo by John Leyba*

time, I know what he really wants is that ring."

Entering the regular-season finale, the NFL's MVP race was between Manning and Minnesota Vikings running back Adrian Peterson. It's possible Peterson became the front-runner after he finished the season with 2,097 rushing yards, second most in NFL history, and powered the Vikings to the playoffs with a 37-34 victory against Green Bay.

But Manning also stamped his candidacy while wearing a Broncos orange-and-blue glove to protect his right throwing hand from the December chill. The glove was more aid than hinderance as Manning completed 23-of-29 for 304 yards, three touchdowns and a robust 144.8 passer rating. In three quarters. Did Michael Jackson get this production out of one glove?

"You know, for wearing it for the first time in my career, I guess you could say it's been OK," Manning said.

It was nearly two years earlier that Manning played in the 2010 season's Pro Bowl, then went down with a neck injury that eventually required four neck surgeries to repair. It forced him to miss the entire 2011 season with the Colts, and led Indianapolis to release him so it could begin anew with a No. 1 draft choice named Andrew Luck.

The Colts' gain was the Broncos' gain. Manning's first regular season with the Broncos is in the books: a team-record 400 completions for a team-record 4,659 yards and a team-record 37 touchdown passes against only 11 interceptions.

"I had no real expectations for what this year would be like," he said. "So I don't know if you can exceed expectations if you never really had any."

Manning led the Broncos to a 13-3 record — not a team record, but their first No. 1 playoff seed since their 1998 Super Bowl team set the franchise record with a 14-2 regular-season mark. ■

Peyton Manning is all smiles after his touchdown pass to Demaryius Thomas in the third quarter of Denver's win over Kansas City on Dec. 30, 2012. In 2012, Manning set Broncos records with 400 completions, 4,659 passing yards and 37 touchdown passes. *Photo by Joe Amon*

Broncos wide receiver Demaryius Thomas goes airborne to grab a touchdown pass in the third quarter against Kansas City. Thomas caught seven passes for 122 yards in Denver's win in the season finale. *Photo by Joe Amon*

CHAPTER 6

Peyton Manning tries to stay warm on the sideline between possessions during the Broncos' second-round playoff game against Baltimore on Jan. 12, 2013. The Ravens shocked the top-seeded Broncos, winning 38-35 in two overtimes. *Photo by Steve Nehf*

A POSTSEASON SHOCKER

PEYTON AND THE GLOVE

Manning Adjusts Well to Playing with a Right-Hand Glove

Maybe someday, Peyton and The Glove will go down with some of more famous player-inanimate object partnerships in NFL history.

Johnny Unitas and the hightops. Lester Hayes and stickum. Jim McMahon and the headband. Conrad Dobler and the bite.

Did you see Manning's stats in the two games after he started wearing The Glove? They've never been better.

Peyton and The Glove.

"I was surprised to see it," Broncos cornerback Champ Bailey said. "Because you just don't see quarterbacks wear gloves. But honestly, the way he's throwing it? I wouldn't be surprised if we do start seeing more of it. I know when I'm just throwing the ball around, I throw better with a glove on."

An older quarterback, if nowhere near an old dog, Manning has shown more than determination and toughness during his remarkable comeback season from four neck surgeries. Those characteristics have been well chronicled.

What has been somewhat underplayed is Manning's willingness, at 36 years old and in his 15th NFL season, to learn new tricks. He has adapted to a new town, a new set of coaches and a new set of teammates, yes. But Manning is renowned for the regimented routine in his preparation.

The Glove on his right throwing hand is an out-of-the-box departure from routine.

"I certainly don't think I would have had to wear the glove had I not been injured last (season)," Manning said. "It's part of my injury, some things that I've had to adjust."

The Glove is not only about what it does for Manning's grip, but what the weather does to the ball.

They go hand in hand.

The colder the weather, the harder and slicker the football. Meanwhile, the most lasting residual effect from Manning's neck surgeries has been the nerve regeneration in the grip of his right throwing hand. In the past, even before the injury, Manning wasn't always at his best in cold weather. Before his injury, he was 1-3 in postseason games played in cold-weather stadiums at New England (0-2), Baltimore (1-0) and the New York Jets (0-1).

But with the temperature in the 30s for the

Peyton Manning wears a glove as he throws during a Jan. 2, 2013 practice at Dove Valley. Manning wore a glove on his throwing hand for the first time in his career in 2012, first adding the accessory in Denver's Dec. 23, 2012, win over Cleveland.
Photo by John Leyba

Broncos' final regular-season game against Kansas City, Manning and The Glove threw for 304 yards and three touchdowns.

The Glove could well be a game changer for Manning.

"No question about it," said Kurt Warner, a two-time MVP who wore a glove on his passing hand the final three seasons of his career. "I know the reason I did it was the idea of getting a little better grip on the football after the injuries I suffered to my hands. So maybe what happened to Peyton is, 'Hey, if I'm a little bit weaker in the hand and these balls get harder and slicker in the cold weather, this might get me back to normal [where] everyone else is.'"

Or get back to zero. This is part of Manning's mental routine when a game or a season isn't going so well. Don't try to get it all back at once. Just get back to zero, he says.

QB Glove's History

McMahon in the late 1980s to early 1990s was the first quarterback to cause a stir by wearing a glove on his throwing hand. As McMahon's career was winding down, Doug Flutie was bringing the throwing-hand glove down from the Canadian Football League, where it's used by many quarterbacks.

Among active NFL quarterbacks, New England's Tom Brady occasionally has worn a glove on his right throwing hand in cold weather, but he usually wears it on his off hand. Pittsburgh's Ben Roethlisberger has been wearing a glove on his throwing hand since his college days at Miami of Ohio.

It was while watching Roethlisberger play on TV that Warner found the glove that aided the second part of his career.

"It took me a long time to work with a glove and really get comfortable with one that I liked," said Warner, who is now a studio analyst for the NFL Network. "Once I did, and even right now, I feel weird throwing without a glove."

The gloves receivers wear have a flypaper-like surface on the inside of their gloves. These are too tacky for quarterbacks. The gloves used by Roethlisberger, Warner and Manning have a softer, old-leather feel on the inside.

"They had a little bit of a tack with more grip, but they weren't sticky at all," Warner said.

Passes Look the Same

Manning began practicing with the glove on his right hand for the week leading up to the Ravens' regular-season game on Dec. 16. He didn't wear it in that game, but the next two weeks he practiced and played with the glove on his right throwing hand.

"I'm sure he's had this all planned out a long time ago," Broncos defensive end Elvis Dumervil said.

Some of Manning's touchdown passes in victories against Cleveland and Kansas City where tight-fit completions to Eric Decker and Demaryius Thomas. Manning's passes don't have any more wobble because of The Glove. They might have had even less.

"I would say there's been no difference in the way he's thrown the ball," Decker said. "It's the same."

And maybe that's the best part of Peyton and The Glove. With the Broncos about to play their first postseason game, with the temperature about to drop well below freezing, The Glove gets Manning back to zero.

"I'm in a different body, some things are different for me," Manning said. "So I've had to adjust." ◾

Peyton Manning calls a play at the line in the third quarter of the Broncos' win over the Kansas City Chiefs on Dec. 30, 2012. Manning wore a glove on his throwing hand against the Chiefs and threw for three touchdowns. *Photo by John Leyba*

OVERTIME AGONY

Manning Calls his Final Pass of Denver's Season a 'Bad Throw'

It had nothing to do with the cold. It had nothing to do with the postseason. It had nothing to do with The Glove.

It had everything to do with committing one of the most egregious sins of playing quarterback — throwing across the body.

Broncos QB Peyton Manning, who by his own admission can't throw the fastball like he used to, rolled right late in the first overtime period Saturday, Jan. 12 and tried to throw back left and complete a pass to Brandon Stokley.

Manning's pass didn't get there. Baltimore Ravens cornerback Corey Graham stepped in front of Stokley and intercepted the ball. The pick set up the Ravens' winning 47-yard field goal early in the second overtime of the second round playoff game.

"Bad throw," Manning said after Denver's 38-35 loss. "Probably the decision wasn't great. I think I had an opening and I didn't get enough on it. I was trying to make a play and (it's) certainly a throw I'd like to have back."

The play was reminiscent of Minnesota quarterback Brett Favre trying to make the same throw late in regulation of the 2009 NFC championship game. Favre was picked off by New Orleans cornerback Tracy Porter and the Saints went on to win in overtime.

For most of the AFC divisional-round playoff game, Manning played well. He threw three touchdown passes, and if Broncos safety Rahim Moore didn't let a Hail Mary-type pass get over his head with 31 seconds left in regulation, Manning would have been a hero.

Instead, Manning committed three turnovers that resulted in 17 Ravens points. Graham picked off a deflected pass in the first quarter and returned it for a touchdown. Manning was strip sacked in the third quarter and the Ravens converted the fumble recovery into another game-tying touchdown.

Manning, who is due to collect $40 million in salary over the next two years, played one more game representing the Broncos before the offseason —the Pro Bowl on Jan. 27 in Hawaii. But even on a frigid day in Denver, palm trees, the Pacific Ocean and warm sunshine didn't sound all that alluring.

"I can't predict tomorrow," Manning said. "I'm just disappointed tonight. It stings — it's supposed to sting, but we'll move from it and move on." ■

Peyton Manning runs off the field after the Broncos' stunning 38-35 loss to the Baltimore Ravens in the second round of the AFC playoffs. Manning's pass to Brandon Stokley late in the first overtime was intercepted by Baltimore cornerback Corey Graham to set up the Ravens' game-winning field goal. *Photo by AAron Ontiveroz*

REFLECTING ON THE GOOD AND THE BAD

Manning Talks Broncos Upset, Looks Toward New York Super Bowl

In a quiet moment outside the Broncos' locker room on Jan. 13, Peyton Manning revealed a peek inside his ever-whirring mind.

Not surprisingly, many of his thoughts were on what he and his Broncos could have done differently to avoid their 38-35, double-overtime playoff loss the night before to Baltimore.

But also true to the Manning mind, the quarterback was buoyed by how the single-digit temperatures that fell upon Sports Authority Field at Mile High enabled him to get a jump on his preparation for the next time he faces such conditions.

"That was another good hurdle for me," Manning said in an interview with *The Denver Post*. "Weather-wise, we had not had anything like that all season. There was some unknown going into that game. You can't simulate it. I tried everything from putting my hand in a freezing tank. But you just can't simulate it.

"Next year, the Super Bowl's in New York. So that was a good hurdle for me to be effective in those type of conditions."

Wait a minute. He put his passing hand in a freeze tank?

Turns out, he can skip the freezer next year. Manning discovered the benefits of wearing a glove on his passing hand this season, which makes him confident the next time the Broncos reach the playoffs — and he did make reference to Super Bowl XLVIII at his brother Eli's home Meadowlands stadium next season — he will be ready for the elements.

Yes, Manning made the fatal quarterback mistake of throwing across his body in overtime. But that was a quick-twitch decision he made after slot receiver Brandon Stokley broke off his route and went back door across the middle.

"I probably shouldn't have done that," Stokley said.

It wasn't the cold's fault the pass didn't get there before Ravens cornerback Corey Graham intercepted it, a turnover that set up Baltimore's game-ending field goal.

The cold's effect also can't be blamed for the pass that deflected off receiver Eric Decker's hands

Peyton Manning waits for a play call in during overtime against the Ravens in the 2012 AFC playoffs. Manning threw for 290 yards and three touchdowns in the loss. *Photo by AAron Ontiveroz*

on the Broncos' first offensive possession and into Graham's arms, who returned the pick for a touchdown.

Manning otherwise played well in the extreme cold, throwing for 290 yards and three touchdowns — including perfect scoring strikes to Stokley and Knowshon Moreno.

It was a performance good enough for a victory until Broncos safety Rahim Moore misjudged a 70-yard flyball with 31 seconds remaining in regulation.

"When you take a year off from football, you come back for all the enjoyable moments," Manning said.

"When you're not playing, you miss out on all the highs, but you also miss these disappointments. But I would rather be in the arena to be excited or be disappointed than not have a chance at all. That's football. That's why everybody plays it. You have to be able to take the good with the bad."

The final evaluation of the Broncos' 2012 season depends on the context from which it is judged. Given a difficult early schedule and the uncertainty of Manning's comeback, a 13-3 regular-season record exceeded expectations.

But after the Broncos earned the AFC's No. 1 playoff seed, expectations were reset. If it helps Broncos fans, Manning feels your pain from the playoff-opening loss to Baltimore. He understands your anger.

"I'll tell you, our fans, they were all-pros yesterday," Manning said. "Sticking through that weather. Loud 'til the end. But no surprise. I always said that about playing here as an opponent, that Denver Bronco fans get it. We're disappointed right there with them.

"I assure you, we worked hard and did everything we could. I know everyone would like to do some things different in the game."

There were way more positive memories than negative for Manning after his first season with the Broncos. But as much as the 11-game winning streak and 37 touchdown passes, Manning will think fondly of his new friendships. With coach John Fox taking the team in a day early for most road trips, a group of veterans formed the Transplant Club. There were Manning, Stokley, Keith Brooking, Jim Leonhard and Joel Dreessen.

"We used to go eat Friday nights, on road games," Manning said. "Decker was the only returnee in the Transplant Club. Coach Fox pointed out he thinks this is the best group of guys he's ever had. It was unique how a bunch of guys came together. We did stuff off the field. We hung out, we got to be friends.

"You can't do it right away, but as the sun continues to shine every morning you do take some time to reflect on some good things that happened this year. It's certainly not the finish that we wanted, but I think it's a mistake if you don't reflect on some of the good things." ∎

Peyton Manning hands off to Broncos running back Knowshon Moreno in the first quarter of the Broncos' second round playoff game against Baltimore. Playing in frigid conditions, the Broncos totaled 125 yards on the ground. *Photo by AAron Ontiveroz*

RECOVERY RECOGNIZED

Manning Wins Comeback Player of the Year, Finishes Second to Peterson for MVP

Broncos quarterback Peyton Manning on Feb. 1 was named NFL comeback player of the year, but Minnesota Viking running back Adrian Peterson won the MVP award.

This was a rare year when the league's two best players — Manning and Peterson — came off serious injuries. Manning missed the entire 2011 season with the Indianapolis Colts because of four neck surgeries. In his first year with the Broncos, he threw 37 touchdown passes against 11 interceptions while leading the team to an AFC-best 13-3 record.

Peterson suffered a torn ACL on Dec. 24, 2011, yet returned this season to rush for 2,097 yards — 8 yards shy of the NFL single-season record set in 1984 by Eric Dickerson.

Peterson also picked up 1,598 of those yards in the final 10 games to all lead the Vikings from a 3-13 record in 2011 to 10-6 and an NFC wild-card berth this season.

Peterson finished second to Manning for the comeback award.

"I used to always say this was an award I never wanted to have, because it meant having a significant injury and missing some time," Manning said. "I will say for any young player out there, if they do get injured I wish they would be as fortunate as I was to receive the kind of help and support from all kind of people from all different places. Denver, Duke University, coaches, trainers, doctors who have supported me. Family members. I'm very grateful to be back playing this game."

Washington Redskins quarterback Robert Griffin III was the NFL's offensive rookie of the year and Carolina linebacker Luke Kuechly won the defensive rookie of the year honor. Colts interim coach Bruce Arians was named NFL coach of the year.

"You just go out there and play, you don't think about the individual awards," Manning said. "You accept them on behalf of your teammates. And so the comeback player of the year, I'd like to thank the entire Broncos organization — the coaches, the players, the support people for helping me get out there and getting back on the field and having a positive return to football." ■

Broncos fans make their choice for the NFL's MVP clear during the Broncos' win over Kansas City on Dec. 30, 2012. Manning finished second to Minnesota Vikings running back Adrian Peterson in the MVP voting, but took home the league's comeback player of the year honors. *Photo by Steve Nehf*

CHAPTER 7

LOOKING FORWARD

Peyton Manning hands off to rookie running back Montee Ball during the Broncos' minicamp on June 12, 2013. The Broncos selected Ball, the former Wisconsin star, in the second round of the 2013 NFL Draft. *Photo by John Leyba*

LIKE A FINE WINE

Broncos' Manning Aging Well

Nobody in the history of the NFL has ever been a better quarterback at age 36 than Peyton Manning. Brett Favre? Nope. Steve Young? No, sir. Johnny Unitas? Please.

The combination of victories and passing numbers posted during Manning's first season with the Broncos were unprecedented for a high-mileage pro quarterback. But know what's even scarier about Manning?

"I think he can keep getting better," John Elway said.

You mean to tell me next season Manning is capable of matching a performance that made him an all-pro in 2012?

"There's no question," Elway said.

As Elway stood in the doorway of the team's locker room on Jan. 16, it was obvious the playoff loss to the Baltimore Ravens still stung the architect of this city's football renaissance. But knowing Elway believes all great NFL teams start with the quarterback, he was asked if Denver can truly expect a 37-year-old Manning to be competitive

with Aaron Rodgers, Matt Ryan or any QB in the league next season.

"No question," Elway said.

Manning won 13 games for Denver. He threw 37 touchdown passes. His QB rating was 105.8, the second-highest mark in a brilliant 15-season career, all of it spent with Indianapolis until the Colts cut Manning.

Elway, however, believes Denver's veteran quarterback can be as good or better in 2013. And the reason might surprise you.

"Knowing Peyton now compared to how I knew him when he first got to Denver, I realize how much tougher this transition really was for him, because of the type of person he is," Elway said.

Pull back the curtain on an MVP-worthy performance, and there was a mess Manning would rather not anybody see. He's an obsessive stickler for detail. As a result, his adjustment to the Broncos was more difficult than Manning made it look when he would drop a pass perfectly in the hands of Demaryius Thomas on game day.

New Broncos receiver Wes Welker (left) and Peyton Manning watch batting practice before the Colorado Rockies-New York Yankees game in Denver on May 7, 2013. With one of the NFL's top receivers in Welker added to the fold, the Broncos are confident heading into the 2013 season. *Photo by John Leyba*

The legend of Elway was built on the improbable comeback. The Drive. He laughed at chaos. No. 7 was a quarterback with a powerful hose for an arm and a fireman's unflappable composure. When the building was burning, Elway walked in. Put out the fire. And nobody even saw Elway sweat.

In maybe 1,000 different ways, Manning is the anti-Elway. Both have Hall of Fame talent. Elway already has been enshrined in Canton, Ohio. There's no doubt Manning will get there. But they have taken vastly different routes.

"For him, the picture of playing quarterback is so much bigger. He looks at so many different things. Everybody's different, but as I look at Peyton now, I realize the transition to a new team had to be huge for him," Elway said.

Manning has the vision to see a safety tip off coverage in a twitch of a leg, or detect a scratch no bigger than your thumbnail on a Buick from 1,000 feet away. No. 18 sweats the big stuff. He sweats the small stuff. From a new team to a new town, every unfamiliar route made Manning uncomfortable until he mastered it.

"I'm not saying it's wrong. Everybody's different," Elway said. "But he likes to know every detail. He doesn't like that building falling down around him. He wants to know every brick in the building. That's his personality. He wants to know everything that's going on. And if he doesn't know it, he doesn't feel as comfortable and he's not as confident."

After four neck surgeries, Manning seems to have made peace with how his body functions. His Denver uniform took time to break in, the same as any guy's favorite pair of jeans.

Arguably no 37-year-old NFL quarterback has been better than Y.A. Tittle was way back in 1963, when he led the New York Giants to the league championship game, only to fall short against the Chicago Bears. So there's the goal for Manning. And you know he will pursue perfection as close to 24/7 as is humanly possible.

When Manning recently revealed he stuck his throwing hand in a freezing tank to simulate playing football in Denver during January, it seemed quirky. But he does everything for a reason. "Next year, the Super Bowl is in New York," Manning said.

It is all the more amazing Manning threw for 4,659 yards for the Broncos, if you know him as Elway now does.

Why? Because you know there were at least 10,000 questions the ever-obsessive Manning had about adapting to Denver.

"A lot of questions got answered for him this season. And he didn't have the answers to those questions before he started here," Elway said. "Now, there's a lot of ways we can help him to make this team better. But he'll come back a lot more comfortable."

The bottom line: It took time, but Manning finally feels at home in Denver.

Now he's ready to hit the road to the Super Bowl. ▪

Broncos executive vice president John Elway, right, introduces Wes Welker during the March 14, 2013, press conference following Welker's signing. The Pro Bowl receiver agreed to a two-year, $12 million deal. *Photo by Hyoung Chang*

A PRESENT FOR PEYTON

Elway Brings Former Patriots Star Welker to Denver

John Elway is 52 years old, walks on an artificial left knee and hasn't played football since Bill Clinton was President. But Elway can still beat the snot out of New England quarterback Tom Brady.

In fact, Elway just did. Hurts, doesn't it, Mr. Brady? Touchdown, Broncos.

Wes Welker scored on a post route so deep it took the five-time Pro Bowler all the way from New England to Denver. He agreed March 13 to join the Broncos as a free agent. Welker was rewarded for switching teams with a two-year, $12 million deal the Patriots were reluctant to give him.

Peyton Manning now has Brady's favorite little buddy as a pass-catching target.

You can hear the chowderheads curse Elway all the way from here in the Rocky Mountains.

This was a good get. It doesn't signal a seismic shift in the balance of NFL power, in the same way the acquisition of Manning did a year earlier. Landing Welker, however, ignited the same fist pumps of celebration at Dove Valley headquarters. Why are those high-fives so significant?

The games on the field belong to the players. But this might well be Elway's favorite stretch of the NFL calendar. This is the time of year that old No. 7 can compete against New England coach Bill Belichick or anybody else in the league with designs on a championship.

For Denver, it's Super Bowl or bust.

You expected anything less, as Manning's window of opportunity closes a little with each passing day?

If it wasn't clear before, there's no mistaking the reality now. Elway is the team architect, but Manning is at the forefront of the boss' thoughts as roster plans are drawn. In fact, Elway has said Manning should have some degree of input in crucial team decisions, the same as Mike Shanahan taking advice from his legendary quarterback when Denver was an elite NFL team.

Manning doesn't want to be the general manager of the Broncos. And the pursuit of Welker was particularly difficult for Manning.

Oh, Manning did place a recruiting call to the Patriots star.

Then, Manning had to make peace with the fact he was pushing old friend Brandon Stokley out of a job.

Wes Welker speaks with the media after a May 20, 2013, practice at Dove Valley. *Photo by John Leyba*

Make no mistake. Stokley is a major reason Manning chose Denver to begin chapter two of his NFL life. Manning is intensely loyal. Football is a tough business, and that's why, for any man with a heart, what makes football sense can also gnaw at the gut.

It appears the Broncos aren't trying to repeat their championship glory years of the late 1990s so much as they are reassembling a very convincing facsimile of the Indianapolis Colts' offense that Manning led to perennial Super Bowl contention.

Denver, which has vowed to play even faster than the 30-point-per-game offensive juggernaut of last season, can now line up Demaryius Thomas and Eric Decker as wide receivers, with Welker in the slot.

Hmm, didn't Manning throw to Marvin Harrison, Reggie Wayne and Stokley back in the QB's Indy prime?

It has been an open secret since the end of the regular season the Broncos would like to upgrade at wide receiver, a move that seemed unfathomable to devotees of Thomas and Decker. While Thomas is on the verge of being a top-shelf No. 1 target, Welker has more than 750 career receptions on his NFL résumé, not to mention talent Decker can't match, with all due respect.

In a league with a salary cap, franchises that win the Monopoly money season know how to legitimately manipulate the budget. While it is overly simplistic to state, there's a kernel of truth to the idea that Elway took $6 million from waived linebacker D.J. Williams and passed it along to Welker. That's cash well spent.

"We wanted to get better. Obviously 13-3 was a successful year, but we lost our first playoff game, so we wanted to take advantage of an opportunity to get better," Elway said. "We'll continue to work on that during the free-agent period and then again in the draft."

Not only did the Broncos improve, they dealt a blow to New England, a consistent Super Bowl contender. Two birds. One stone.

Wonder how Brady feels now, after the glamour-boy quarterback restructured his contract for the purpose of keeping the Patriots on top during the twilight years of his NFL career.

The Manning vs. Brady rivalry has always been intensely competitive.

This is only a guess: The rivalry between the Broncos and Patriots just got hotter.

C'mon, Belichick.

Give us a scowl. ▪

New Broncos receiver Wes Welker carries the ball after making a catch during the Broncos' minicamp on June 12, 2013. In 2013, Demaryius Thomas and Eric Decker are expected to line up as wide receivers, with Wes Welker in the slot. *Photo by John Leyba*

Broncos backs (from left) Jacob Hester, Montee Ball and C.J. Anderson run through drills during the last day of Broncos minicamp on June 13, 2013. Rookie running backs Ball, a second-round pick out of Wisconsin, and Anderson, an undrafted free agent out of Cal, are vying to join fullback Hester in the Broncos' backfield in 2013. *Photo by John Leyba*

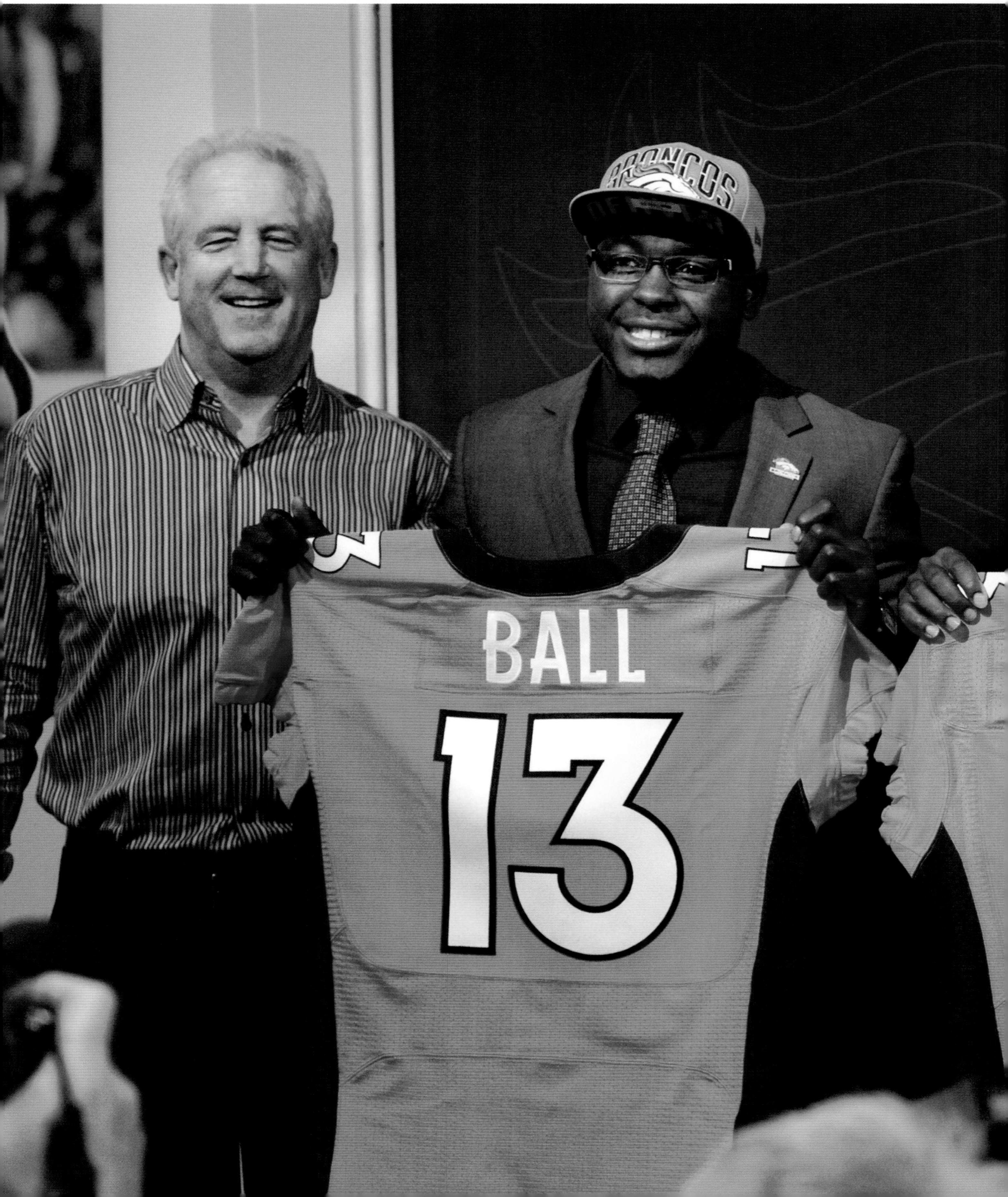
BRONCOS
BALL
13

Broncos coach John Fox, left, and vice president of football operations John Elway introduce draft picks Montee Ball and Kayvon Webster during an April 27, 2013, press conference. Running back Ball was selected in the second round and Webster, a cornerback, was taken in the third round.
Photo by Craig F. Walker

A PURPOSEFUL VACATION

Manning Serious About Football After NFL Offseason

It used to be when America went on vacation, Mom and Dad packed up the station wagon, told the kids to shut up and drove off to an exciting, never-before-seen destination a whole state or two away.

Peyton Manning just finished his vacation that included a USO Tour to Afghanistan, a $500,000 donation to the foundation of his college's former women's basketball coach, delivering speeches on leadership to several corporations and accepting awards in New Orleans and Kansas City, Mo. And he got in three days of passing with his new receiver Wes Welker and returning targets Demaryius Thomas and Eric Decker at Duke University.

"I wouldn't call it a summer vacation," Manning said.

Such is the jet-setting life of a star NFL quarterback — a star quarterback who happens to be employed by the Broncos for going on a second season.

Manning and most of his Broncos teammates returned to work April 15 for the start of the team's offseason conditioning program at the team's Dove Valley headquarters.

For Manning, the workouts are a welcome break from his offseason vacation. He and the Broncos last played Jan. 12, when they were upset 38-35 in double overtime in frigid conditions at home by the Baltimore Ravens.

"I think it's still a motivating factor for this season," Manning said. "We did some good things last year, but did not finish the way we wanted to. We lost our last game of the season, which there is really only one team (that didn't). I don't think that San Francisco is any happier than we are because they played in the Super Bowl. Baltimore is really the only team that probably had the most enjoyable offseason."

Enjoyable isn't the best way to describe Manning's offseason. But it was purposeful. Was he this busy during his early career offseasons? He didn't just sign a check to the Pat Summitt Foundation for the benefit of Alzheimer's disease; Manning also co-chairs the board.

Brett Favre would put on Wranglers and drive a tractor around his Mississippi ranch.

Peyton Manning throws a pass during drills at the Broncos' minicamp on June 12, 2013. Manning was excited to begin preparing for the 2013 season after an eventful offseason. *Photo by John Leyba*

Manning puts on a suit and tie and motivates corporate executives.

"February and March are two good months to kind of fulfill some commitments that you have to do," he said. "The USO Tour was something new for me. It was truly a life-changing trip. I really enjoyed the experience meeting some of the great men and women in our military. I've always tried to fulfill some of those commitments so that when the off-season program does begin, you can take care of the football workouts and our meetings and be uninterrupted that way."

He mostly gave his much-scrutinized right arm a rest until last week. After spending all of his 2012 offseason rehabbing from the affects of four neck surgeries, then attempting 626 passes, 40 of which went for touchdowns, in 17 games, 13 of which resulted in victory, Manning pretty much shut down his 37-year-old arm and body until March.

Arriving at the Duke campus in Durham, N.C., on Monday, April 8, Manning threw timing routes and worked out with his two favorite returning receivers, Thomas and Decker, and his newest target Welker on Tuesday and Wednesday. Manning and Welker, who spent the previous six seasons with the rival New England Patriots, stayed over for another passing and route-running session Thursday.

"I think he's gotten a little stronger, but I can't really say, because (last year was) my first time playing with a quarterback like Peyton," Thomas said. "It was fun this past year, because I'd never had balls come at me like that. I can't say much about the strength of his arm, because I never really played with him the years before he got hurt. I think it's the same." ■

Peyton Manning speaks with reporters after practice during the Broncos' organized team activities on May 20, 2013. Motivated by the team's upset loss to Baltimore in the AFC playoffs and the Broncos' signing of wide receiver Wes Welker, Manning is optimistic heading into the 2013 season. *Photo by John Leyba*

Photo by AAron Ontiveroz